Camp Borden
A Century of Service

1916-1918

1919-1939

1939-1945

1946-1970

1970-1990

1993-2016

BORDEN
E PRINCIPIO

William A. March
and Terry A. Higgins

Camp Borden
A Century of Service

Text by William A. March © 2015-2016

with additional material by Terry A. Higgins © 2016

1st English Edition, Base Borden Military Museum
in association with Aviaeology Publishing © 2016

ISBN 978-0-9780696-2-9 (softcover)

ISBN 978-0-9780696-7-4 (hardcover)

Project Leader • LCol Stuart L. Beaton, CD (Retired)

Design, Layout, & Production Management
      • Terry Higgins, SkyGrid Studio / Aviaeology Publishing

Designed, Printed, & Published in Canada

Published by the **Base Borden Military Museum**

27 Ram Street

CFB Borden, Ontario

Canada L0M 1C0

(705) 423-3531

Email: stuart.beaton@forces.gc.ca

Library and Archives Canada Cataloguing in Publication

March, William Anthony, 1959-, author

    Camp Borden : a century of service / William A. March and Terry A. Higgins. -- 1st English edition.

ISBN 978-0-9780696-7-4 (hardback).--ISBN 978-0-9780696-2-9 (paperback)

1. Canada. Canadian Forces Base (Borden, Ont.)--History.

2. Air bases--Ontario--Borden--History. 3. Borden (Ont.)--History.

I. Higgins, Terry, 1962-, author II. Base Borden Military Museum, issuing body

III. Title.

UG635.C22C345 2016   358.4'170971317   C2016-902101-7

Published in association with **Aviaeology, by SkyGrid Studio**

123 Church Street

Kitchener, Ontario

Canada N2G 2S3

(519) 742-6965

Email: info@aviaeology.com

www.aviaeology.com

Preface

This was not an easy book to write.

For one hundred years Camp Borden has been part of the Canadian military landscape. During that time it has become an integral part of the history of the country, the province and the local counties. Thousands of men and women who have passed through Borden's gates have gone on to the serve the nation in peace and war leaving their mark on the Camp in countless ways. Families have called it home, even if for the short period of time that makes up a military posting, creating stories and memories of their own. Units have come and gone; some with the startling rapidity that is a hallmark of military life, while others have resided at Borden for decades and each has a rich history of its own. To put it simple, the history of Camp Borden is too large a tale to be captured in a book of this size.

So the reader should consider this but a taste of the sumptuous banquet that is Borden's story. Commissioned by Lieutenant-Colonel Stuart Beaton (Retired), the Director of the Base Borden Military Museum, the book commemorates one hundred years of a very unique institution, but it does not tell the complete tale. There is much more work to be done. And an excellent starting place would be a visit to the Military Museum, and its Air Force Annex, where one will discover elements of Camp Borden's history that could not be covered in so slim a publication. Reaching out and touching one of the armoured vehicles in the Major-General Worthington Memorial Tank Park, or visiting the restored First World War training trench, will give the visitor a concrete link to the words in this book.

Wrinkles and all, Camp Borden is still going strong and will "soldier on" for many years to come. The landscape may change, buildings will come and go, and its role will adapt to changing times, but the men and women who are the heart and soul of Borden will see to it that the camp continues to serve Canada with honour. The stories that will fill the next chapter of Borden's history are even now being written.

Enjoy the read.

Major William A. March, CD
Trenton, Ontario,
March 2016

Table of Contents

Namesake:
Sir Frederick William Borden, KCMG, BA
MD (1847-1917), Canadian Minister
of Militia and Defence 13 July 1896 to
6 October 1911.

A sudden stop for JN-4 (Can) "Canuck" No. C335. Training accidents were a common occurrence during the early days of flying operations at Camp Borden.

Why Borden?

For most of its history Canada has relied upon a small, permanent army supported by a volunteer reserve known as the militia. Formed around units with local ties to an area or community, militia members were organized, equipped and paraded as deemed appropriate by the government of the day. On paper the militia companies, battalions and regiments, along with support elements, would in time of dire need be brought together to form brigades and divisions. However, the scattered location of militia units, combined with the cost of bringing them together for large-scale training, meant that "militia concentrations" were nominally held once per year at a suitable location. Most of the militia camps were located on property that had been used for military purposes since the War of 1812 and were not of a size to accommodate the large numbers of troops expected to take the field in a modern war.

Prior to The First World War Canada had been divided into 12 Military Districts (MDs) with each MD responsible for the training and administration of the units within its boundaries. Militia District No. 2, with its headquarters located in Toronto, Ontario, conducted its summer concentrations at the Niagara-on-the-Lake camp, located just outside the town of the same name. By 1904, the space available at this camp was no longer deemed adequate and the Minister of Militia and Defence, Sir Frederick William Borden, directed that steps be undertaken to find a more suitable training area. Although a number of possible locations were examined, interest quickly focused on an area north of Toronto, near the village of Angus.

Located in the township of Essa, Simcoe County, approximately 18 kilometers (km, or 12 miles) west and south of the city of Barrie, Angus was a collection of but a few houses in 1905. The land around the town had once been covered with pine forest, but heavily and sustained logging had reduced it to "a sea of stumps." Two independent assessments were undertaken both of which indicated that although it would take substantial effort to build a camp, the land was suitably flat, had available water resources and was reasonably near rail lines. The land was deemed "not of use for much else" and could be acquired for an estimated $47,000 with much of this amount recouped from the sale of the more economically valuable Niagara-on-the-Lake property. Unfortunately, just when it looked as if a decision was about to be made to acquire the necessary land, objections were raised by parties who wished to keep militia training, with its somewhat lucrative local economic benefits, in the Niagara area. No decision was forthcoming and MD 2 was forced to make due with its existing facilities.

Although the need for a new, better training camp was raised periodically after 1905, nothing came of it. Not even the start of The First World War spurred the need for a change in how things had always been done despite the dispatch to Europe of the Canadian Expeditionary Force (CEF). Still, as early as April 1915 the Federal Government had acquired some parcels of land in Essa township, but there was no firm plan to establish a military facility. It was not until 1916, with Canada's pledge to "do more," and the need to replace casualties from the disastrous Somme offensive, that pressure mounted once again for a new camp. Sir Sam Hughes, a somewhat eccentric and controversial individual who had replaced Borden upon his election defeat in 1911, visited the area around Angus on 7 May 1916 and decided "on the spot that the best site for the camp would be in the township of Essa." The following day Hughes informed the Privy Council that "it is imperative that a suitable training area should forthwith be acquired for the training of the troops now being mobilized in…Western Ontario, who numbers will comprise, approximately, twenty thousand men." Four days later, on 11 May 1916, the Government of Canada approved the estimated $174,183.32 it would cost to appropriate the necessary land. Camp Borden, for Hughes had decided as early as 2 May to name the new facility after his predecessor and close friend, was now a reality.

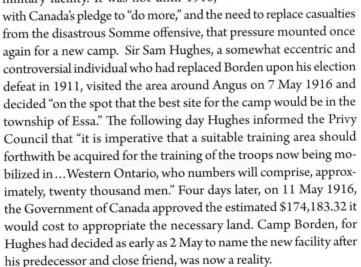

LAC PA-066782

The caption for this British and Colonial Press photo says "Canada shortly to have the largest military camp in America. Twenty thousand acres near Barrie, Ont., bought by the Dominion Government at a cost of £300,000."

Establishing the Camp

Eventually 7163 hectares (17,700 acres) of land within the townships of Essa and Tosorontio (also in Simcoe County) were acquired. The site, known locally as "The Plains" was located on a vast, level plateau approximately 229 meters (m, or 750 feet) above sea level with the Mad and Pine rivers, tributaries of the Nottawasaga river, cutting across the landscape. Although complete government approval for the establishment of a camp greatly accelerated the efforts of the Purchasing Agents, the need to have troops training at Borden by the summer of 1916 made the building of the necessary facilities quite urgent.

The services of Bate, McMahon and Company were obtained to build the camp. The company was experienced, had been on the current government's list of "preferred contractors" since 1911, and had as its General Manager, "Lieutenant-Colonel" R.A. Low, one of Hughes' multitude of honorary colonel appointments. This well-connected company had worked on the hastily built camp at Valcartier, Quebec, that had housed the initial contingent of the CEF in 1914. Work was carried out under the supervision of military engineers and was to be on a cost plus percentage basis. The speed at which everything was to be ready precluded the preparation of detailed plans or specifications and no thought was given to putting anything out for public tender; after all there was a war on. By the end of the year, an eye-brow raising $1,206,361.21 had been authorized for Borden.

Below: Work on the foundation of the Army Service Corps freight sheds, showing a steam-powered concrete mixer in operation. This photograph shows over $25,000 worth of machinery at this one point of the big camp alone.

Below right: Work gangs were transported to and from the various construction sites by truck.

Within days of obtaining the contract, Low had 500 men working in two 12-hour shifts at various sites. The first military presence at Borden was a small security section of seven stalwart individuals who were to guard the mountains of construction supplies. They were quickly joined by two companies of the 157th (First Simcoe) Battalion that were immediately tasked with clearing stumps upon their arrival on 16 May. Six weeks after construction commenced full strength military units began to arrive at the camp.

The project was massive. The camp was to be laid out in the shape of a long, narrow city. A central main street about 3.6 km (2 ¼ miles) in length and 6.7 m (22 feet) wide was constructed out of concrete to handle heavy traffic. Side streets, each .8 km (½ mile) long, jutting out periodically at right angles, were 5.5 m (18 feet) wide and paved with rock asphalt macadam to handle lighter traffic. These main thoroughfares were to be lit by 150 electric, nitrogen-gas lamps placed at 61 meter (200 foot) intervals.

There was an abundance of pure water available at Borden. Five artesian wells were drilled to an average depth of 33.5 m (110 feet) and between them provided a flow of 7,955,658 litres (1,750,000 gallons) per day. The water was distributed throughout the camp via 24 km (15 miles) of wrought-iron mains and there were over 15,000 taps for various purposes as well as three hundred shower and bath facilities. An up-to-date sewage system met all of the camp's sanitary requirements.

Left and below: Road building in progress. Steam power and horse power were ubiquitous presences at every heavy construction site throughout the massive project. With the road-building still in progress, the electrical infrastructure, in the form of power lines and street lamps is already taking shape.

Below left: A Toronto fire engine provides the pumping power for temporary water supply.

Above: The distribution and pumping station and motors inside the station on 26 October 1916.

Permanent buildings, such as the camp headquarters, quartermaster stores, and recreation facilities, lined the pave streets. There were built using "gunite" (injected cement) permitting the rapid addition of cement floor, walls and roof to a wooden superstructure. Temporary or less important buildings were of wood-frame construction, covered with a "rubberoid" (artificial shingles) roofing. Troops undergoing training would be housed in tents.

And then there were the training areas. A rifle range consisting of 400 targets with firing points out to 549 meters (600 yards) was built, along with "live-fire" areas for machine guns and artillery. Numerous parade squares were laid out to teach proper military decorum and strict adherence to commands through hour upon hour of "square bashing." Eventually several kilometers of trenches would be added to permit new soldiers to be exposed to the latest in trench

text continued on page 7

Right: Targets at the rifle range shortly after construction in 1916, and later, the range in use by the Machine Gun Section of the 129th (Wentworth) Battalion under the direction of Lieutenant Shearer, with their Lewis guns.

(far right) British & Colonial Press photo
LAC PA-066799

Left: The platform area of the Grand Trunk and Canadian Pacific Railway stations at Borden on 11 July 1916.

Right: Corporal CH Harvey with Privates FC Pierson, M Hamilton, DJ Reynolds, M Martin, T Carter, and J Pearson of the 157th Battalion — some of the very first arrivals in the summer of 1916.

LAC PA-051586

"Canada's Greatest Military Review" was the national headline of the day — Three cheers for his Majesty the King led by General "Sam" Hughes (right) at the review at Camp Borden of 30,000 Canadian troops.

LAC PA-066773

Another view of the reviewing party during the grad opening of Camp Borden on 11 July 1916.

warfare tactics before they experienced the real thing in Europe. All of these training areas were linked together by kilometer after kilometer of dirt roads – perfect for route marches and pack drill.

Even working round-the-clock, utilizing modern equipment and construction techniques, and employing soldiers as required as extra manual labour, it took months to complete all of the necessary construction. Regardless of the actual state of completion, Sir Sam Hughes and associated dignitaries attended the official opening of Camp Borden on 11 July 1916. More than 30,000 men were then housed under canvas awaiting training at that time. They would be part of a massive parade, nine brigades strong (34,000 soldiers), who stood under a hot summer sun while they were reviewed by Hughes and his entourage. For many of those watching the parade it seemed that "the thirty-four marching battalions [were] purposely dragging their feet to send as much as possible of the ubiquitous sand and black wood ash (from pine stumps burnt to clear the land) directly onto Hughes and his retinue on the reviewing stand."

Training was hard. Most of it was designed to "toughen" the men up and to expose them to the rigours of military discipline. The powers that be seemed to think that route marches and drill (and more

drill) was the best way to instill marshal prowess in the battalions. Long hours were also spent on the ranges honing marksmen skills and learning the intricacies of the various machine guns that were dominating the battlefields of Europe. As the war progressed, training at Borden became more sophisticated as the realities of trench

warfare were brought back to Ontario by veteran instructors. Practice trenches built to resemble the elongated earthworks of Europe became classrooms where assault tactics, raiding and gas drills were taught. It was not easy, yet by the end of the war approximately 300,000 soldiers had been trained at Borden.

The Royal Flying Corps and the Royal Air Force

Although the airplane became a true weapon of war during The First World War, Canada's major contribution to the fighting was the CEF. There were attempts to form a Canadian service through that conflict, but all Canadian flyers served with either the Royal Flying Corps (RFC), the Royal Naval Air Service (RNAS), or after the amalgamation of these two organizations on 1 April 1918, the subsequent Royal Air Force (RAF). Borden's involvement arose out of the rapid expansion of the RFC in late 1916 brought about by the need to meet a growing demand for more squadrons in the field and to replace higher than expected casualties from air combat. Air authorities in England viewed Canada as a prime location to establish a training organization that would give it access to a perceived large pool of flying trainees and equipped with Canadian supplied aircraft and engines.

With general details agreed to between the Canadian and British governments, authorization was given on 21 December 1916 to establish a training organization in Canada that would consist of a number of squadrons, training facilities, aerodromes, recruiting

A class in artillery observation in progress at Camp Borden in 1917.

LAC PA-022775

CB2007-0444-02

offices and administrative facilities. Material and engineering support would be provided by a newly formed Aviation Department of the Imperial Munitions Board to be located in Toronto. Aircraft and engines were provided via a combination of purchases abroad (primarily in the United States) and from Canadian Aeroplanes Limited, Toronto. Selected to oversee it all on behalf of the RFC was Lieutenant-Colonel (LCol) Cuthbert G. Hoare.

Above: RFC Headquarters building, Armour Heights, Toronto, Ontario.
Top: Group photo of 82nd Canadian Reserve Squadron, Royal Flying Corps, Borden, May 1917.

Lieutenant-Colonel Hoare (by the end of the war he would be a Brigadier General) and his advance party arrived in Toronto on 22 January 1917. Canadian military authorities suggested that Borden would be an excellent location at which to establish a training aerodrome. Hoare, accompanied by the General Officer Commanding MD 2, Major General W.A. Logie, travelled via rail to Angus to visit the site – it was not to be an auspicious start to Borden's aviation "career."

Heavy snow closed the spur line from Angus to Borden and it took Hoare's party nearly two hours to cover the five mile distance by sleigh. Although snow-covered the recommended site, not too far from the main army area, had great potential as it had access to an existing sanitary system, power plant, water supply and railway siding. As far as Hoare could tell the ground under the snow seemed flat and adequate for flying purposes. Furthermore, the Canadian government offered 405 hectares (1000 acres) to the RFC free of charge. Hoare, who envisioned a flying operation of some five squadrons, up to 90 aircraft and 1,500 all ranks, was anxious to get started. He signed a contract to build the flying facility on 27 January with the same Colonel Low and company that had built the military training camp at Borden.

Eight days later the rail line to Borden was again open and a work force of 400 men descended on Borden removing stumps and undertaking preparatory work for upcoming construction in freezing temperatures. Within a week, the number had grown to 1700 working through the night under light provide by giant electric arc lights. Six weeks after he signed the contract most of the 15 hangars were complete and there were suitable buildings available for headquarters staff to take up residence on 16 March. They would control and administer No. 42 Wing consisting of five Canadian Training Squadrons (Nos. 78 – 82).

Built almost literally from the ground up, the RFC Canada (after 1 April 1918, RAF Canada) was a massive undertaking that would eventually consist of three Wings (Deseronto and North Toronto being the locations for Nos. 43 and 44 Wing respectively), five active airfields (Rathburn and Mohawk for No. 43 Wing, Leaside and Armour Heights for No. 44 Wing) of which Borden was the largest, and twenty training squadrons. Initially training at Borden focused on the basics of flying, but as the RFC Canada matured the squadrons located there began to specialize in the more demanding areas of instruction. No. 80 Squadron concentrated on aerial gunnery, while No. 78 exposed students to wireless telegraphy and Nos. 79, 81 and 82 taught the basics of formation and cross-country flying, as well as aerial photography. Soon the sound of a JN-4 overhead became commonplace in the skies over Angus and Barrie and, unfortunately, the sight of an aircraft upended in a farmer's field also became a regular addition to the landscape.

Hoare officially took control of the aerodrome at Borden on 2 May 1917, but construction continued for another month. By mid-June the work teams, under the supervision of Royal Engineers, had cleared 344 hectares (850 acres) of stumps, laid 7.6 kilometers (4 ¾ miles) of macadam road, installed 6.9 kilometers (4 1/3 miles) of water mains, 1493.5 meters (4900 feet) of sewers, heating and incinerating facilities, electric power distribution systems, and under-

Above: The impressive hangar line was a dominant feature of the RFC /RAF aerodrome side of Camp Borden.

LAC PA-022776

Far left: A JN-4(Can) "Canuck" stunting over the hangar line at Camp Borden. This very "graphic" photographic image has the appearance of a piece of darkroom trickery, but the surprise expressed in the body language of the ladies and gentlemen on the ground suggest otherwise.

Left: An aerial view taken from a JN-4 looking south over the hangar line and busy aerodrome Camp Borden in 1917.

Left and above: An RFC machine gun trainer and RFC trainees practicing with a Thornton-Pickard Mk. III H machine-gun camera. Right: RFC students learning how to spin a propeller.

ground storage tanks for gasoline. Fifty-seven buildings, including the hangars, were erected and so well built were they that some of them remain in use 100 years later. Cognizant of the need to look after their personnel during off hours, the RFC elected to add such amenities as a swimming pool, golf course, sports fields and a track. Of prime importance was the levelling and seeding of the aerodrome proper since aircraft in those days operated almost exclusively from grass strips.

Training had begun long before the construction had been completed. The first Canadian trainees reported to Borden on 28 March and two days later they were undergoing instruction on Curtiss JN-4 aircraft assembled at the camp. A two-seat aircraft with a robust airframe, almost all of the military pilots trained in North America at the time did so in this aircraft. The instructor sat in the rear cockpit, while the student sat in the front. Given the nature of most aircraft accidents (i.e. nose first), the front seat was usually the most dangerous. Training flights were often scheduled for early in the morning or late in the day to take advantage of the relatively calm winds.

Initial flights were often of short duration, measured in minutes, and until the introduction of the systematic

Gosport Training System, little instruction was provided on the theory and science of flight. Instead, the instructor gave the student a "feel" for the aircraft with the student's first solo occurring after scant hours in the air. After the student's first flight on his own, some additional instruction was provided, especially on specialist squadrons, but for the most part the student was expected to "learn by doing." Often they were encouraged to try their hand at "stunting;" simple aerobatics today, but quite dangerous then. Borden suffered its first flying fatality when Cadet J.H. Talbot was killed in a flying accident on 8 April; he would be the first of some 129 cadets and 20 instructors who lost their lives by accident there. "Wastage," as these losses were often referred to, was an accepted part of military aviation.

The initial course of 40 cadets graduated from Borden in June 1917. By the end of October they had been joined by a further 1041, plus 72 American pilots (51 for the United States (US) Army and 21 for the US Navy). The training of American airmen came about after the US entry into The First World War on 6 April 1917. Lacking the facilities and personnel to train the large number of pilots that would be required, the Americans approached Britain for assistance who gave

the task to RFC Canada. General Hoare saw an opportunity. Long worried about how he would ensure that training continued during the often severe Canadian winter, he traded his organization's experience for the use of American airfields in Texas. Therefore, towards the end of October 1917, No. 42 Wing moved virtually its entire operation by train southward, not to return until early April 1918.

Those that remained at Borden, as with the other aerodromes in Ontario, experimented with winter flying by employing skis on the JN-4's and figuring out how to keep fluids from freezing in flight. They also adopted many unusual forms of dress to keep from freezing to death in the open cockpits during flight training. Although not always successful, these early experiments paved the way for year-round flying in Canadian conditions.

The End of the War

For most people and governments the end of The First World War came unexpectedly. Plans had already been laid to continue the conflict into 1919, so when the Armistice was declared on 11 November 1918, there was a period of somewhat confused "business as usual." Flight training at Borden continued, as did militia training. Then everything began to wind down very quickly.

Training ceased abruptly and individuals who were under instruction were demobilized as fast as could be. For a time the facilities were used to house Canadian personnel returning from Europe until it was their turn to take off their uniform and return home. Then there was the need for additional hospital beds during the Spanish influenza epidemic in 1919.

Where possible, surplus equipment and stores were disposed of. Aircraft that a few short months ago were vital to the war effort could be obtained for as little as $50. Furniture and other day-to-day items were sold in lots or became the fodder for numerous sales to the public. Buildings on the military portion of Borden were retained by the Department of Militia and Defence, at least for the time being, but those around the aerodrome were the property of the United Kingdom. By Order-in-Council, the Canadian government purchased them in 1919 at a cost of $375,000.

Still, it was not long before Borden became a virtual ghost town with a small caretaker contingent to undertake routine maintenance and look after security. This period of inactivity did not last long. Already individuals concerned with the future of aviation within the country were looking at the facilities that the government had just acquired. A new lease on life was mere months away when once again the skies would resound to the roar of aircraft engines.

LAC PA-056197

Left: The wreckage of JN-4(Can) No. C136 at or near Camp Borden in 1917.

Below: A Royal Air Force ambulance at the ready in 1918.

Below left: Mosaic map making is demonstrated in this circa 1917-1918 photo at Camp Borden.

LAC PA-022781

2

The Interwar Period: 1919 - 1939

Captain McEwen with Avro 504K G-CYAC, one of the first two aircraft to be registered with the Canadian Air Board on 18 June 1920.

DND HC33

Right: Canada's most decorated serviceman, fighter pilot Major WG Barker, VC, DSO & Bar, MC & two Bars, is in the rear seat of this Avro 504K at Hounslow Aerodrome in the United Kingdom in April 1919, where he commanded an RAF fighter training school. Back home from May 1919, after a stint in the aviation business, now LCol (Wing Commander equivalent) Barker served as the Station Commander at Camp Borden from 1922 to 1924. In those early years, the Avro 504K was the most prolific pilot training aircraft in Canada.

DND M-839 D

Cradle of Military Aviation

At the very end of the war an embryonic Canadian Air Force (CAF) had been formed in England. Comprising one fighter and one bomber squadron, the CAF never saw combat and the flying units were disbanded within months. The primary duties of CAF personnel in England became the dismantling, packaging and shipping of over 100 surplus aircraft the United Kingdom gave to Canada. Similar "Imperial Gifts" were provided to the other British Dominions as well in the hopes that they would help foster aviation within the respective countries. These donated aircraft changed the history of Borden.

During the first week of January 1920, Flight Lieutenant (F/L) G.O. Johnson and a party of nine men arrived at Borden via sleigh to re-activate the old RAF Canada camp. They started with the hangars and work spaces opting to live in Angus and commute, regardless of the weather, back and forth. Crated aircraft arrived periodically via train and were transferred by horse-drawn sled to the hangar line where a "triage" was undertaken to determine what was useful (some of the material had been damaged in transit) and to prioritize the reassembly. The work was sporadic in nature dependent as it was upon the arrival of cargo trains. During periods where there were no aircraft to work upon, the men concentrated on getting the quarters and mess facilities up and running. By February 1920 all personnel were permanently located at Borden.

The reassembled aircraft were tested and either retained at Borden or shipped to various CAF operations. By now a civilian Air Board had been created to guide initial development of aviation in Canada and the CAF was the non-permanent, military arm of this body. Personnel were employed as civil servants by the Air Board and appointed to the CAF at various rank levels. Most of the work undertaken during this period involved providing refresher training at Borden, demonstration flights to emphasize the utility of aircraft, or making the first forays into the type of missions (forestry patrols, etc.) that would lead to the "bush pilots in uniform" nickname for early military aviators in Canada.

Work on the aircraft at Borden progressed rapidly and the first of many, an Avro on skis, was flight tested in March. Two months later, almost all of the aircraft had been received. The first "student" to undergo refresher flight training, J.S. Scott, completed his training on 16 August 1920. The following month, perhaps in recognition of the steady increase in CAF personnel, Ottawa agreed to form No. 1 Wing to oversee training. Flying units consisted of a school and No. 1 Squadron with a scout (fighter) flight operating Royal Aircraft Factory Scout Experimental SE.5a aircraft and a bomber flight (which also provided night flying training) equipped with de Havilland D.H.9A's. A ground school was formed that provided instruction in engine repair, aircraft maintenance, wireless telegraphy, photogra-

Above: The CAF Motor Transport Section at Camp Borden in 1921.

DND RE-13830

Above right: Royal Aircraft Factory SE.5a, G-CYAY (ex RAF F9114) as it entered service with the Canadian Air Board at Camp Borden in 1920.

DND DRM-1071

Right: The aftermath of the accident to de Havilland D.H.4a, G-CYAN, at Camp Borden.

DND RE-15914

phy, gunnery and navigation. Support sections, such as motor transport and quartermaster stores, were also established. Camp maintenance was placed under the charge of a small cadre of civilian employees. Airmen, most of whom had wartime experience, were put through their paces re-learning old skills. By the end of the year 86 officers and 111 other ranks were considered trained. Pilots, all of whom were to be reserve members of the CAF, had been given a minimum of flight time, averaging a mere six hours and six minutes per candidate.

The year 1921 was an important one for the CAF. Although more civilian than military in employment and organization, the military side of the Air Board pressed to be allowed the use of an ensign to denote its role as an arm of the defence forces of the Dominion. There had been some discussion with respect to creating a "Canadian" ensign, but instead permission was sought to use the RAF ensign in recognition of both the bond between the two services and the war-time service of many of the CAF. On 30 November 1921, the ensign was hoisted aloft at Borden during a parade attended by 45 officers, 169 airmen and several Avro 504s in the air.

Post-war reorganization was completed in 1923 and with it came the creation of a new Department of National Defence (DND) and the disbandment of the Air Board; the CAF was now subordinate to the Chief of the General Staff. The first new pilot trainees arrived at Borden and although 30 students had been expected as part of the Provisional Pilot Officer programme, only nine showed up on 15 May 1923. This disappointing start to the training year coincided with discussion on whether to keep Borden open as the cost of heating and maintaining the buildings, only a fraction of which were used by the CAF, was deemed excessive. Even Mother Nature seemed to be signalling that the old RFC camp should be abandoned as a major wind storm on 23 May, although it lasted only

twenty minutes, damaged many of the buildings and hangars. Long Branch on the outskirts of Toronto was considered as an alternate location, but the facilities available were in even worse shape than those at Borden. So the decision was made to remain.

Part of the discussions surrounding the formation of DND was whether or not a permanent Canadian air service should be formed. With the dissolution of the Air Board, the CAF became responsible for the control and guidance of both civil and military aviation in Canada. The increased responsibility resulted in a decision to place a portion of CAF on regular (full time) status. It was placed under a director and made subordinate to the Chief of the General Staff. In recognition of the wartime service of Canadian aviators a request was made in 1923 for permission to use the "Royal" sobriquet. Approved by King Edward VII, the Royal Canadian Air Force (RCAF) came in official being on 1 April 1924. Its formation was celebrated with an appropriate parade and flypast at its home – Borden.

1924 and Beyond – the Royal Canadian Air Force

Borden remained the principal air base of the RCAF until a second major station was opened at Trenton in 1931. Very little in the way of purely military training was carried out as the RCAF concentrated on producing aircrew to fulfill the requirements of Civil Government Air Operations, such as forestry and fisheries patrols, with the occasional Arctic expedition thrown in. Technical training focus on what was required to keep the modest, and aging, aircraft fleet in the air. The majority of flying and ground courses where conducted at Borden with the graduates dispatched to various air stations throughout the country. However, if you stayed in the RCAF it was virtually guaranteed that you would spend an inordinate amount of time in Borden.

text continued on page 19

The first Ensign raising ceremony at Camp Borden on 30 November 1921. In the far left photo, an Avro 504K, G-CYCB performs a smart low-level flypast on the occasion.

DND RE-15463 and RE-15462

The Ensign is about to be unfurled for the first time during th 1921 ceremony.

DND RE-15465

General views of the Wing Repair Section at Camp Borden during the winter of 1920 - 21 showing various component parts of Avro 504K aircraft undergoing rework and repair. *DND RE-15972 and RE-15975*

The sole occupant of this Avro 504K, S/L K. Tailyour, killed when flight testing it just after it was assembled on 11 April 1921. The experienced flight instructor was performing a roll at low level at the time. *John Griffin collection*

Others were not so serious — ski-equipped Avro 504K G-CYDA suffered a Category C accident with F/L HS Quigley at the controls on 23 January 1922. It was repaired and later configured as a floatplane. *DND RE-15965*

Above: First World War fighter ace and former Newfoundland Regiment soldier (Gallipoli veteran), F/O Roy Grandy with the experimental army co-op airborne radio displayed in a Camp Borden JN-4 in 1922. He would leave the Air Force the next year and return in 1925 after a short stint as a commercial aviator. Like a number of the other instructors, and some of their students, at Borden, Grandy would go on to become a key figure in the RCAF, serving in various squadron, wing, and station commander roles through into the Second World War. He retired, having attained the rank of Group Captain, in 1946.

the Terry Higgins collection / Aviaeology archives

Above right: Entrants in the new Officer Cadet Training Program at Camp Borden in the late summer of 1923. Second from the left in the back row is C.Roy Slemon undergoing flying training on the Avro 504K as a member of Provisional Pilot Officer Training Course No.1. He was later to become Air Marshall Slemon, Chief of the Air Staff and Deputy Commander of NORAD, and on retirement the Executive Vice-President of the U.S. Air Force Academy. *DND PL-117804*

Right: Together with the Sopwith Camel, the SE.5a was considered to be a top-shelf fighter aircraft. Of the dozen "Sees" taken on strength at Camp Borden in 1920-1921, G-CYBJ pictured here, would become the first accident write off when it suffered structural failure on take-off, 21 October 1920. *GR Hutt via the John Griffin collection*

Given the RCAF's broad aviation mandate, many of the courses were attended by civil personnel as well as members of the Army and Navy. Almost all of these courses were undertaken during the summer months to take advantage of good flying weather. During the winter aircraft only a modest amount of flying was conducted as mechanics and riggers tore the aircraft down and put them through a rigorous maintenance programme. Life at Borden was somewhat isolated as there were very few vehicles amongst the RCAF personnel and the town of Angus had little in the way of diversion. Recreational facilities at the camp were well used and sports, such as hockey and baseball, were popular. Sojourns to the big city of Barrie were few and far between, often centering on official functions and parades.

The growth in aviation in Canada spurred a 1927 government reorganization that led to the creation of separate branches to look after Civil Government Air Operations, Engineering and Technical Services, and a Comptroller of Civil Aviation. The RCAF, al-

though a separate branch, would retain a role in all of these areas, but the reorganization permitted the service to focus more of its efforts on defence requirements such as training with the army. One outcome of this undertaking was the purchase the following year of nine Armstrong Whitworth Siskin fighters and six Atlas army co-operation aircraft, from the same company. Unfortunately, opportunities to work with the army were few and far between, but the Siskins were most useful as a public relations tool. Based out of Borden, the Siskins made their first large scale public appearance in 1929 at the Canadian National Exhibition and were a big hit. The Siskin Flight would go on to perform at air displays across the country stimulating an interest in aviation.

By 1930, slow but steady growth resulted in an RCAF strength of approximately 174 officers and 669 airmen. Almost half of this number was employed supporting civil operations throughout the country with the majority of the remainder at Borden. The training wing located there now included a Flying Training Wing consisting of

text continued on page 26

A product of the explosive growth as an army and air training facility during the First World War, Camp Borden remained the largest airfield in Canada for some years to come. By the time this early 1920s photo was taken the nascent Canadian Air Force had not yet become the Royal Canadian Air Force. In the year after the RCAF came into being, Camp Borden would become No. 1 Flying Training Station — the only station dedicated to training full time — with the establishment reorganization that was authorized in Privy Council on 19 May 1925.

The Ground Trades

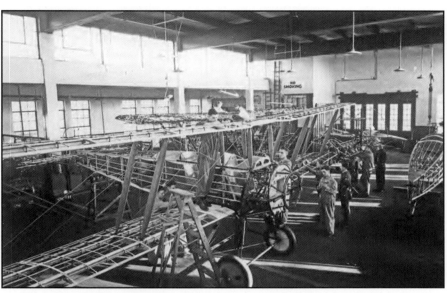

Camp Borden was more than just a flying trades training facility of course. Here future riggers (airframe technicians) undergo classroom instruction with an Avro 504 airframe and drawings as teaching aids.

...while on the same airfield, others practice the craft learned. In this hangar, an Avro 504N and, beyond it, an Armstrong-Whitworth Atlas are the subject of Station Repair Flight structural inspection and repair.

In the shops... At left, the engine repair and overhaul shop with a line-up of what appear to be Avro 504K rotary engines on workstands, and at right (central to page), parachute packing in progress. Both taken at Camp Borden in the 1920's.

engine shop image, DND RE-15453

...and the sheds. The ample hangarage at Borden served as a storage facility for the large Felixstowe flying boats that were part of the Imperial Gift of First World War surplus aircraft from Britain. They were transported by rail to the seaplane stations on an as-needed basis. This photo was taken 30 March 1922.

The Cradle of Canadian Military Aviation ...

Above: A Hucks Starter being brought up to an Avro 504N trainer, circa 1928.

Left: A quiet sort of hero, the Leyland Ration Truck equipped with railroad wheels was used for winter ration pick ups in Angus when the roads were closed.

Above: The results of a hastily aborted take-off by P/O H Carefoot on 9 December 1929 ended up in this dramatic pose, and the write-off of Avro 504N No. 51.

Left: Sometime earlier than January 1928 shows a lineup of Avro 504N's and older 504K's at one end of hangar row. The write-off victim shown above would have been aircraft 'CD (G-CYCD) at the time.

DND PL-117076

Left: Communications equipment at camp Borden circa 1936. Note all of the radio call signs affixed to the wall.

CB2007-0444-32

Although a military airfield, Camp Borden would also play host to civil aviators from time to time. The odd looking Fokker C.II (based on the famous wartime D.VII fighter) seen in the above photo was operated by the US firm Brock & Weymouth who did contract survey work for Canadian National Railway using this Canadian registered aircraft in the mid to late 1920's.

DND RE-18656

Three de Havilland D.H.60 Moths, one of them airborne, and a pair of Fleet Fawns at Borden airfield in 1936. The Moth had replaced the Avro 504N as the primary flight training type at Borden some five years earlier.

CB2007-0444-01

Fighters

RAF Armstrong Whitworth Siskin Mk. III J7758 in the midst of cold weather trials at Camp Borden in 1926. This was one of two subsequently purchased by the RCAF (separate from the new purchases of 1928). J7758 was lost in a fatal crash while being flight tested in the hands of No. 2 Squadron on 28 June 1927. *DND PL-117076*

Former RAF Siskin Mk. III J7759, now serial number "10" as a "new" RCAF fighter, on the flightline at Camp Borden in the company of three new Siskin Mk. IIIA's, an Atlas army co-op aircraft, and a Fairchild cabin monoplane utility aircraft, circa 1928-1930. J7759 was the second of two RAF Siskins that had arrived in Canada for the purpose of cold weather trials in 1926. *DND RE-16931*

Above: Siskin Mk. III J7759 has all the appearances of a fresh new arrival in this circa 1926 photo. *LAC PA-066479*

Left: RCAF Siskin Mk. IIIA No. 22 and pilot are prepared for a winter flight, circa 1928-29. An optional ski landing gear was a mandatory requirement of all RCAF aircraft types of the period. This aircraft has the Thornton-Pickard Mk. III H machine-gun camera installed on the upper wing, suggesting that the pilot may be heading out for a stint of air combat practice flying. *DND RE-16621*

Army Cooperation

RCAF Atlas Mk.I G-CYZB was one of four of the type that were taken on strength at Camp Borden in the week or so few days of 1927. Others would arrive in the summer of 1928. In early June 1928 this aircraft had its markings changed to the two-character serial No. 16, which was changed again to No. 401 by late November 1936.

DND RE-11619-1

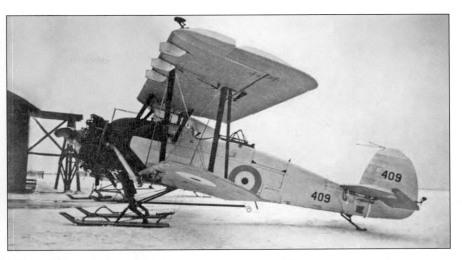

RCAF No. 409, a later-delivery (1934) Atlas Mk. IAC, is seen here on ski landing gear at Camp Borden, in the late 1930s. These aircraft were usually based at Trenton or Rockcliffe by then, so this was likely a training or liaison flight. Earlier Atlases, like 'ZB in the photo at left, were later converted to the Mk. IAC configuration with the smaller-area "all rudder" vertical tail. Atlas '409 was struck off RCAF strength 13 September 1939, thee days after Canada declared war on Germany.

CB2007-0444-04

DND RE-11619-3

With her message pick-up hook deployed, Atlas No. 19 practices message retrieval on the airfield at Camp Borden. The big "M" on laid out on the ground, the two rifles bayonetted into the dirt as posts to hold the pick-up line, and the observer's daring do in the rear cockpit were all a standard part of the technique. This aircraft was later used to test floats for the type, before being renumbered 404 in early 1937. After stints at both Trenton and Rockcliffe, Atlas 404 was with No. 118 (Coast Artillery Cooperation) Squadron at St. John, New Brunswick when it actually sortied in search of a reported U-boat, but returned in bad weather with engine trouble.

Pilot Officer (P/O) E.A. McNab (right) with Flight Lieutenant David A. Harding and P/O Edwin McGowan at Camp Borden 3 September 1929. As the new decade arrived, flying demonstrations given all across Canada with the wonderfully aerobatic Siskin (in the background) had become one of the duties carried out by these and other capable young RCAF officers. *DND PL-117106, via the Carl Vincent collection*

Avro 621 Tutors on skis ready for winder flying training circa 1928-1929. The photo was taken on orthochromatic film, which gives the overall yellow paint scheme good contrast against the snow. *the Carl Vincent collection*

Above: An Avro Tutor during a sports day at Borden. F/L "Ack" Lewis takes up Corporal Jock Cameron for a parachute jump. In the coat, S/L "Soup" Campbell, and next to him is F/L Ross.

Left: Civilians examining a Tutor line-up during sports day, circa 1934. These aircraft have now by now been converted to the army co-op role with new radio equipment and a message pick-up hook installed under the belly.

three squadrons, and a Ground Training Wing with three schools. However, the growing cost of keeping the old buildings functioning, perhaps highlighted by a fire that destroyed the officers mess that year, led the RCAF to press for a new, modern base to be located at Trenton. No sooner had the decision been made, and construction started, then the world entered the Great Depression.

The Great Depression of the 1930's hit Canada hard and government retrenchment became the order of the day. During the "Big Cut" of 1931, the RCAF had its budget reduced by almost fifty percent and one-fifth of its personnel were let go. Military activity at Borden was reduced to a minimum while men from the local area, as part of government relief programmes, found work at the camp replanting trees for the princely sum of fifteen cents an hour plus board. Hangars were used to store aircraft for which there was no money to buy fuel.

Nevertheless, Borden did offer some things that could not be replicated at Trenton; wide open space, gunnery and bombing ranges, and accommodations for the Army. In 1932, the School of Army Cooperation was formed offering courses of varying length during the summer. This was to be the bread and butter of the RCAF

at Borden for the next three years until the deteriorating international situation led to a renewed emphasis on defence – especially air defence. Beginning in 1935, modest budget increases allowed the RCAF to undergo a limited expansion which meant increased training at both RCAF stations. Within the year a new training group was established at Borden along with air armament, technical, flying and navigation training.

In the years leading up to The Second World War, Borden became the "summer home" for RCAF auxiliary squadrons as they underwent summer training. By 1938, the RCAF, now a separate service with a senior air officer reporting directly to the Minister of National Defence (MND), began to allocate more and more funds to Borden. New bombing and gunnery ranges were constructed and the months leading up to the war saw a flurry of building activity. A contract for eight new buildings, the first major structure erected since The First World War, was awarded to the Frontenac Construction Company of Kingston, Ontario. These red tile and wood buildings included a new officers mess, staff quarters, drill hall, technical stores and a barrack block. The work began in August, mere weeks before Germany invaded Poland on 1 September 1939.

Below Left: Men struggle to combat the fire that destroyed the Officer's Mess in 1930.   *DND RE-13532*

Below: A Fairchild FC-2 "Razorback at Camp Borden. The official caption gives the date as 1927, but it is most probably the summer of 1928. The RCAF had replaced its civil aircraft letter character markings with two character numbered serials in January 1928. Siskin No. 22 is present in the background, as is the sole surviving RAF machine, J7759 which has yet to have its orignal markings changed.

Where was the Army?

It is safe to say that for the majority of the inter-war period, Borden was an air base. Although it had been a major training location for the land forces during the Great War, lack of funds precluded the gathering together of a large number of units to take advantage of the facilities located there. As well, there was little money available for other than the most basic of maintenance, resulting in a gradual decay of buildings and infrastructure.

Some militia units, especially those located nearby, did make occasional use of Borden, but only for brief periods and in small numbers. As well there were infrequent "cooperation" courses offered for artillery and air force members. The only permanent army presence was that of the Royal Canadian Corps of Signals (RCCS). In the early 1920's, a Signal Depot was opened at Borden located within a few of the "temporary" huts left over from the war. There was a need for a small regular detachment (Permanent Active Militia) to be co-located with the CAF (and then the RCAF) to provide wireless training for air personnel. A growing need for additional signallers, stemming from the opening in 1923 of radio stations in the Northwest and Yukon territories, resulted in the opening of a permanent RCCS school in 1926 under the command of Lieutenant Colonel "Bonnie" Weeks.

For more than a decade, the RCCS and small militia elements were the sole Army presence at Borden. By the mid-1930's Canada was slowly beginning to increase its defence forces and Army headquarters needed to find training facilities to accommodate the anticipated growth. Unfortunately, as noted by the Chief of the General Staff in a letter to the Deputy Minister in 1938, "funds expended on maintenance had for some time been cut to the lowest possible figure, and barracks, armouries and militia properties generally had deteriorated to a considerable degree as a result." Once again, the Army would have to "make do."

Borden was one of the "militia properties" that had suffered due to lack of funds. Yet the Army needed the training space that the camp had in abundance. In May 1938, it became the home of Canadian Armoured Fighting Vehicles School (CAFVS). Tanks had been introduced on the battlefield in The First World War, but Canada had only begun to organize a tank corps of its own when the conflict ended. Rapid demobilization had ended this initial foray into armoured warfare until 1930. The purchase of twelve tracked machine gun carriers led to the hasty creation of a course in Kingston. When a lack of instructors placed this initiative in jeopardy, Captain Frank Worthington, or "Worthy" as he was often called, a veteran of the 18th Machine Gun Brigade of the CEF, stepped forward and filled the gap, learning even as he taught the first course.

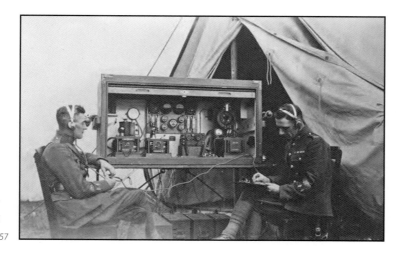

RCCS wireless between Ottawa and Borden was maintained with "portables" such as this one seen at Borden in 1921. *LAC PA-092357*

The Tank Corps, twenty-three all ranks, with Worthy as its first Commanding Officer, was initially located at London, Ontario. When training and maintenance space proved inadequate, it was transferred to RCAF Station Trenton, but this proved to be only a minor improvement. Eventually, the Corps found its new home in one of the unused hangars at Borden. Brevet Lieutenant-Colonel Worthington was now responsible for training six active militia units on the intricacies of armoured operations utilizing the original twelve carriers and whatever additional vehicles he could acquire or manufacture.

August and September 1938, saw the first large scale training concentration held at Borden in years. Over four thousand men, primarily permanent force units augments as required by local military battalions, came together to train. It was an all arms (infantry, cavalry and artillery) exercise that focused on a defensive battle reminiscent of the last war with emphasis on "digging and wiring." Two RCAF squadrons, Nos. 2 and 3, provided aerial support while the CAFVS joined in towards the end of the exercise. By the end of the second week of September the visitors had gone home and Borden readied itself for another winter.

Yet not all of the Army troops went home. Small elements of the Royal Canadian Engineers, Signals, Service, Medical, Ordnance and Postal Corps remained or arrived over the next few months. Some took up residence to support the armoured school, while others began the herculean task of resurrected some of the buildings and training areas. More arrived during the summer of 1939. The start of The Second World War found the Army population at Borden to be a robust 28 officers and 226 men. They were the first of thousands. 🌲

Upper left: Royal Canadian Dragoons troops rest their horses at the bivouac, Camp Borden, 1938. *DND PMR81-386*

Lower left: Horse lines at Regimental Headquarters, and "B" Squadron, Royal Canadian Dragoons, at a bivouac near Schomberg during the march from Toronto to Camp Borden, 1938.
DND PMR81-387

Below: A Royal Canadian Dragoons patrol, Camp Borden, 1938. Note the "tin hats" and antenna on the truck (indicating the presence of communications equipment) as the Canadian Army prepared for a "modern" war.
DND PMR81-384

3

The War Years: 1939 - 1945

Australian student pilots in discussion over a map on the tail of a Harvard trainer at RCAF Station Borden, circa 1940-41. *DND PL-4038*

29

Humble, but fundamental beginnings: Course No. 1 of the CAFVS ran at Camp Borden from 11 to 23 July 1938 and most, if not all, graduates would go on to either fight in The Second World War, or train others in subsequent armoured warfare courses. A small number of Carden-Loyd Machine Gun Carrier Mk. VIs (pictured flanking the men in the photo) and Vickers Mk. VIb light tanks were the only armoured vehicles in the Canadian Army inventory at the time. Twelve members of the Windsor Regiment (RCAC) are among the Course No. 1 students pictured.

Mustering as to War

Canada declared war on Germany on 10 September 1939. It had been decided that two complete divisions, plus support troops, would be mobilized as part of Canada's war effort. This placed a premium on available training space and Borden once again topped the list of preferred locations. The Officer Commanding MD 2, Colonel S.A. Lee, whose headquarters still administered Borden, wrote Ottawa on 9 September once again brining the deplorable condition of Borden to the attention of the MND.

The situation at Camp Borden is very unsatisfactory. The very small strengths of C.A.F.V.S. and R.C.A.S.C. Training Centre make the question of protection of Government property extremely difficult. There are insufficient personnel to carry out this duty, and it entails a very severe strain on all ranks. This situation should improve if the home war establishments, when approved, are adequate.

However, it would be several months before the situation was rectified.

Initial emphasis was placed on preparing the First Canadian Division so that it could deploy overseas as quickly as possible. It would be filled by the best available personnel from permanent and militia units. Plans for Borden centred on training those cadres that would make up the Second Division. An ambitious building scheme was being drawn up, but major construction would not commence until the spring of 1940. During the remainder of 1939, troops busied themselves with lectures and technical training conducted, when possible, in the warmth of existing buildings.

Construction workers poured in to Borden during the first quarter of 1940 and for a while it seemed as if there were as many civilians as there were military personnel. In May, at the peak of the initial building program, almost 1500 were employed, assisted and guided by 600 personnel from the Royal Canadian Engineers under the command of Capt. C. Bermingham. Borden was still envisioned as a "summer camp" with the bulk of the training taking place outdoors from April to October. Therefore, construction would focus on preparing ranges, administrative and quarters for staff, as well as recreational, medical and dental facilities. The last elements destined to be part of the First Division, nine officers and 546 men, departed for Europe 11 May 1940. Within a few weeks they would be replaced by an estimated 10,000 trainees representing 20 different units.

Construction started before the last of the winter frost disappeared and even the occasional unexpected heavy snowfall did not slow things down. Teams surveyed and staked out sites for anticipated arrival of the various units while civilian labourers cleared and prepared the land. Almost before this task was done, Engineers and contractors began to build permanent and semi-permanent buildings at each location. A tank range, eagerly anticipated by the now more than 1500 men of the Tank Corps, was finally completed and

"Father of the Canadian Armoured Corps", Col Frederic Franklin Worthington, MC, MM, CD, (centre), then OC of the CAFVS at Camp Borden with Lt Col Mason (left) and Major Gow of the Windsor Regiment. This photo is believed to have been taken just before the start of The Second World War. "Worthy", or "Fighting Frank" to some, was a seasoned mercenary prior to The First World War and later a decorated veteran of the Canadian Machine Gun Corps (MC at Vimy, 1917). He earned his rise through the interwar ranks as an ardent student of armoured warfare, becoming its chief proponent and specialist in Canada. In the postwar Army, he trained initially on the Carden-Loyds at Borden in 1930, and later, in 1936, on heavier equipment at Bovington, UK. He returned — followed soon by Canada's first dozen tanks, the Vickers Mk.VIb's, which he helped in acquiring — in 1938. His keen "mercenary mind" was likely a key instrument in the later acquisition of 265 surplus US M1917 (licence-produced Renault FT's) light tanks for use as training vehicles.

Arrival of the ex US Army M1917s at Camp Borden in October 1940. The message chalked on the nearest vehicle is "Good Luck Canada / Take 'em Away".

DND WRC-373

work on extensive rifle and machine gun ranges, to be the largest in eastern Canada, commenced. In the administrative centre of the camp structures housing headquarters staff, maintenance facilities, messing and quarters for officers and men, and even a blacksmith shop went up seemingly overnight. An effort was even made to brighten up the location with the planting of maple and elm trees. By the end of May approximately 230 new buildings had been erected.

Armoured Beginnings

Camp Borden's first war-time Canadian Army Commanding Officer (CO), perhaps due to the fact that the Armoured School was the largest unit at the camp, was Colonel Worthington. His tenure lasted from April until 28 May 1940 after which Brigadier General R.O. Alexander took up residence as the new CO. Arriving at around the same time were an advance party of 15 officers and 296 other ranks (ORs) who had the responsibility to prepare the way for the units undergoing training. The first of these regiments, the 1st Hussars and Lord Strathcona Horse arrived on their heels. Other units, mainly from the Toronto and southern Ontario region quickly followed.

As each arrived they were assigned a unit area that had been allocated to them in advance. Each had its own washroom and toilet facilities, kitchens, headquarters and buildings for storage and training. The men were housed in tents and most of the training would be conducted in the open air. Even church services, the first of which was held on 26 May by His Grace Derwyn T. Owen, the Anglican Archbishop of Toronto, were conducted outside. In all, there were five unit-areas each capable of accommodating a battalion size group of 800 all ranks, plus 11 slightly smaller locations for groups of 500 personnel or less. The largest of the training spaces could handle up to 1500 trainees undergoing instruction on infantry procedures and tactics.

DND WRC-375

DND PMR-81-383

Infantry and armoured training would dominate the Army portion of Borden during the war years. Most of the soldiers had already completed basic instruction prior to their arrival and were given advanced instruction at Borden prior to proceeding overseas. In addition to physical conditioning and the inevitable parades, men were taught bayonet fighting, how to handle machine guns and automatic weapons such as the Bren, Sten and Tommy guns, and the safe use of hand grenades. Long hours were spent on the rifle ranges interspersed with time spent digging weapons pits, fox holes and the proper placement of wire entanglements. So many personnel arrived to be trained that facilities thought to be adequate were overwhelmed and improvisation became the order of the day.

DND WRC-371

Above left: Worthington inspecting the newly arrived training tanks, the purchase of which was made to look like a business-to-business scrap iron deal on paper, in the interest of bypassing any US Neutrality violations. DND WRC-375

Above: Scrap iron in training!

Another view of the unloading of the Renaults from rail flatcars.

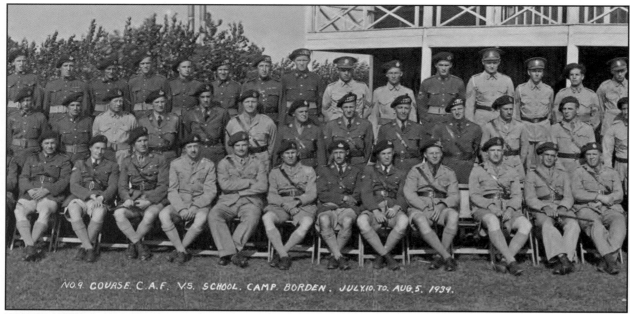

NO. 9 COURSE. C.A.F. V.S. SCHOOL. CAMP. BORDEN. JULY.10.TO. AUG.5. 1939.

LAC MIKAN-4473994

DND ZK-45

Above left: No. 9 Course of the CAFVS graduated on 5 August 1939. Each Course took a month or so to complete at the time, as war loomed on the horizon. Actual tanks had yet to be used at the school.

Above: Major Gordon Churchill of The Fort Garry Horse — the first unit to use the "Renaults" at Camp Borden. The American Renaults which had been purchased at less than $200 a piece in 1940, were put to good use until 1943.

Left: The father of Canadian Armour, Major General Worthington later in his career with the much more capable Ram (a Canadian derivative of the American M3) in the background.

Far Left: The emblem of the later Royal Canadian Armoured Corps, which was born under Worthington's watch as the Canadian Armoured Corps.

Land Force Training Expansion

Canada's land forces, both for service overseas and as part of the Home War Establishment, continued to grow and with this increase came the need for year-round training. The initial concept of Borden serving as a summer training facility went by the wayside and the summer and fall of 1940 saw additional construction at an even more hectic pace. Plumbers, tinsmiths, bricklayers, roofers and general labourers, some 3500 in all, worked to erect barracks to house trainees during the cold winter months and instructional facilities, including 12 drill halls, to permit year-round activity. By end of the year, the number of new buildings at Borden totalled 750 including a 75-bed military hospital allowing for the establishment of a detachment of the Royal Canadian Army Medical Corps.

With progress being made on the camp proper, attention was paid to the recreational requirements of off-duty soldiers. The Canadian Legion moved into the World War I Young Men's Christian Association (YMCA) building, while the YMCA waited for new accommodations to be built. The Salvation Army and Knights of Columbus also took up residence at Borden. Theatres, recreation halls, and canteens were erected to entertain the troops, along with a brand-new detention centre for those who transgressed military law. A brand new post office was also installed to handle the mountains of mail coming in to, and going out of, the camp.

When Brigadier General G.E. McGuig arrived in December 1940 to take command, Borden was a small city growing in leaps and bounds. Vehicles were arriving in ever increasing numbers, including additional training tanks for the Armoured Corps. Advance course in anti-aircraft operations, a ski school and commando courses were being organized. The ski school proved extremely popular, despite a rash a minor injuries. In February 1941, courses on tactics, intelligence, sniping, range finding and provost duties were added. That same month the Canadian Infantry and Canadian Machine Gun Training Schools were stood up.

So many courses were being run, involving so many trainees that the Armoured Corps began to complain that their range areas were being overrun. The RCAF, which used a large open parcel of land for bombing practice, was approached for permission to utilize this strip of land when not being used by the Air Force. An agreement was quickly reached and the Tank School began to erect targets in the new training area. By now armoured training in Borden was developing along two paths: the first focused on providing reinforcements for the various reconnaissance battalions, and the second concentrated on providing additional personnel for the tank brigades.

Camp Borden from the air in the early 1940s. On the Army side of the base (central in the photo) clumps of "tent cities" show as neat arrays of white dots, while at least 18 aircraft can be seen along hangar row in the lower left on the Air Force side. *DND PL-648*

Opposite page: a small sampling of the scores of units that flowed through the training establishments at Camp Borden in late 1940.

Borden is one of those delightful places in Ontario where there can be extreme variation in the weather. Records for heat were broken with the temperature often toping 34 degrees Celsius (94 degrees Fahrenheit). Training exercises were marked by numbers of men collapsing from the heat and there were long lines to be endured for a warm shower at the end of the day or a quick dip in one of the pools. Activity continued at a hectic pace throughout the fall, but after an all too brief Christmas leave period, Borden experienced one of the worst ice storms in memory in January 1942. The temperature fell to minus 32 degrees Celsius (minus 25 degrees Fahrenheit) and stayed at that level into February. The risk of frostbite and exposure severely limited training and just when it seemed that it was starting to warm up, a massive blizzard struck the camp making roads impassable and curtailing range activity due to drifting snow. Although the Engineers were driven to the point of exhaustion trying to keep the over 65 km (40 miles) of roads open, the Armoured Corps delighted in the opportunity to trial new equipment, such as motorized toboggans (we would know them as skidoos).

Throughout 1942, additional training establishments and schools were created. Anticipating a requirement for additional military police once the invasion of the European mainland had begun, a Canadian Provost Corps Training Centre was stood up on 19 February. As well, anticipating that German forces might resort to gas warfare, defensive training against this potential threat grew in size and scope throughout the year. And as more and more personnel began to arrive at Camp Borden the available space, especially for live fire and employment of heavy vehicles, began to get crowed. Therefore, it was decided that additional property was required to serve primarily as an armoured and artillery training area.

In the fall of 1942, the Canadian government purchased a large block of land along Georgian Bay. Approximately 6,800 hectares (17,500 acres) located northwest of the town of Meaford was allocated for the purposes of tank and artillery training. The Meaford Military Camp, or Camp Meaford, would become the focal point for armoured training for many years to come. However, during the Second Word War the primary training facilities remained at Borden

A Christmas-card perfect picturesque view of Building A-65, the Canadian Armoured Corps Training Establishment NCO's Quarters, on 12 December 1941 at Camp Borden. *LAC PA-05162*

while manoeuvre and live-fire ranges were located at Meaford. Beginning in November 1942, trainees and equipment would shuttle back and forth between the two camps as required.

Camp Borden was, by 1943, one of the largest training areas in the country and, especially after Canadian troops engaged in combat on a large scale with the invasion of Sicily on 10 July, one of the busiest. Not only was there a requirement for more troops to replace losses, but there was a need to adapt training to include the latest combat techniques and procedures. The Camp continued to grow with well over 1000 buildings either in use, under construction or in the design phase. Just under 20,000 troops could be housed in various barracks, while during summer training phases another 2,500 could be accommodated under canvas. Infrastructure improvements kept pace with the installation of additional roads, water chlorination and distribution facilities, sewer pipes and lighting. Garbage was treated, burnt, or fed to very appreciative pigs belonging to a local farmer.

Recreation facilities were also important to provide physical training and diversion for the large numbers of young men transiting through the camp. The largest military theatre in Canada, capable of seating 5,200 people, showed the latest in Hollywood movies. Indoor and outdoor swimming pools, sports fields, hockey rink and gymnasiums were built and utilized both as training facilities and

text continued on page 38

REINFORCEMENT COY. 2ND CANADAIN PIONEERS R.C.E. CAMP BORDEN AUG. 1940

LAC MIKAN 4473781

1ST BATT. Q.O.R. N.C.O.s CAMP BORDEN AUG. 1940

LAC MIKAN 4474484

No. 5. ESSEX SCOTTISH. REC. COY. CAMP BORDEN. OCT. 31st 1940.

LAC MIKAN-4474346

No.1 C.I (R) T.C. No.2 R.C.R. COY. CAMP BORDEN. OCT.23 1940.

No.1 A.C.R. (REG) COY No.1 C.I "A" T.C. CAMP BORDEN AUG. 1940

for a growing sports programme. A base library and education centre provided additional diversion and the opportunity to improve one's general education. And yet, despite all that Camp Borden had to offer, every weekend hundreds of young Canadians would make their way to nearby Barrie to sample, albeit briefly, all of the social activities available in a war-time community.

Throughout 1943, the Canadian troops continued to fight in the long and costly Italian campaign. Then, in June 1944, other Canadian divisions landed in Occupied France. Just prior to the Normandy invasion, Major-General Worthington was placed in Command of Borden for a second time. To him fell the responsibility to train replacements for casualties resulting from combat operations, as well as meeting the requirement to inculcate the latest fighting techniques. More emphasis on the basics, such as marksmanship, anti-tank weapons and all-arms manoeuvres, became the name of the game. Added to the already substantial training areas was a miniature village to teach rudimentary tactics for street fighting which was taking such heavy tool of Canadian soldiers in both France and Italy. The last full year of the war saw almost 33,000 personnel pass through Borden's training facilities.

While fighting still raged in Europe during the early months of 1945, training facilities in Canada were being reorganized and downsized. For Borden, especially for armoured training, this meant an increase in both staff and trainees as outlying facilities were closed. Training continued at its normal hectic pace and when Victory in Europe (VE) Day was declared on 8 May 1945, some units in the field on exercise did not get the news that the European war was over until that evening when they returned to the main camp. Although the country was still at war with Japan, there was a general sense of relief as both military personnel and civilians celebrated and gave thanks.

Recruiting throughout Canada came to a halt. Training at Borden continued, but there was uncertainty with respect to the size of Canada's contribution for a Pacific war. As well, during the summer more and more men were returning from Europe and part of the Camp was set aside as temporary housing and re-integration facili-

An unidentified crew commander in a Ram Cruiser II tank at the Canadian Armoured Corps Training Establishment on 7 July 1943.

DND Z-1757-2

ties. Finally, on 15 August it was announced that the Japanese had surrendered and the Second World War was over. Celebrations started early and continued until late at night with no more than the usual trouble to be dealt with by military and civilian police. Camp Borden was now at peace.

From September 1939 until August 1945 Camp Borden had been at the forefront of the Canadian war effort. Almost half the overseas army, approximately 185,000 military personnel, had received all, or part, of their training at Camp Borden. Now the big questions were "When can I go home?" and "When are they going to shut the Camp down?" These were questions to be answered by Ottawa and dealt with by Major-General M.S. Dunn, who had taken over from Worthy in March 1945. Dunn would remain at his post until 1948, guiding the Army portion of Camp Borden to an uncertain peacetime future. *text continued on page 41*

Camp Borden - Army training underway…

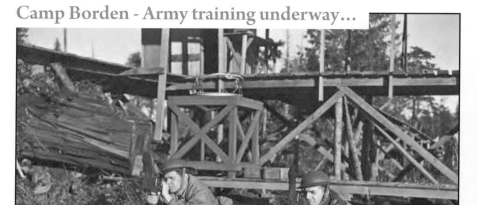

Clockwise, from the left:
Issutrated in the first two photos are Army trainees in small arms training — the bayonette lunge technique and Bren gun practice firing.
DND PL-14 736 and PL-14729

Incoming! And going "to town" on leave or to the next assigned base? The number of Gray Coach Lines buses at Borden in this 4 April 1941 photo gives a good impression of the Camp population at the time. *LAC PA-054698*

Demanding motorcycle operator training underway for commandos and dispatch riders, circa the summer of 1943.
DND ZK-516

Field activity included demolitions training with explosives. In this dramatic image, note the proximity of the brave motorcyclist trainee (at the central left edge of the photo) to the explosion.

Armoured vehicle training underway using Ram Cruiser tanks at Camp Borden in early July 1943. Crews destined for active overseas units would usually go on to models of the somewhat similar Sherman tank on the combat fronts.

DND ZK-518

ZK-315

DND ZK-305

ZK-308

W/C Frank S. McGill, a key figure in the RCAF's training operations, became the first CO of No. I SFTS at Borden in 1940.   *LAC MIKAN-4324947*

Below: The RCAF Station Borden portion of the larger Camp Borden complex, looking north along hangar row in the winter of 1941-42. The vast field of snow to the west is marked with the many criss-crossing tracks indicative of aircraft activity. The town of Angus lies beyond the woods in the upper right part of the frame near the photo aircraft's wing struts.   *DND PL-49*

And on the other side of Camp Borden – the RCAF

When Canada declared war on Germany on 10 September 1939, RCAF Station Camp Borden was one of two major air force bases in Canada (the other being Trenton, Ontario). A centre for air force flying and technical training, it was home to the Intermediate Training Wing Headquarters, Intermediate Training Squadrons, an Intermediate Ground Training School and No. 2 Technical Training School. The RCAF was already in the midst of a modest expansion and when news arrived of the government's declaration, the Station was immediately placed on a war footing. A small contingent of the Irish Regiment of Toronto arrived to serve as a guard force for the air force compound.

Work continued on a number of projects that had been started that summer, but the impetus for future growth came with the signing of the British Commonwealth Air Training Plan (BCATP) agreement between Canada, the United Kingdom, Australia, and New Zealand. Recognizing the importance of air power, these nations implemented a programme that would turn out tens of thousands of trained aircrew by the end of the war, and Borden would have a major role. The agreement was signed on 17 December 1939, but in the preceding months Borden was already a beehive of activity.

For the next year, the key word at RCAF Camp Borden would be "more;" more buildings, more runways, more aircraft and more facilities to meet the training requirements driven by the BCATP. Three paved runways, which would become synonymous with the Plan, were put in place just to the west of the old RFC hangars. Work commenced at the end of October and was completed six weeks later. The First World War hangars continued to house the aircraft, but they were soon joined by new barracks, quarters, kitchens, dining facilities and instructions spaces.

The most immediate need in the RCAF was for instructors with which to man the various Service Flying Training Schools (SFTS) and advanced schools. The existing Flying Instructors Flight was enlarged to school status in November and given the daunting task of churning out instructors at the rate of 54 every four weeks. These graduates would become the initial cadre of BCATP instructional personnel.

The sheer scope of the Plan called for a reorganization of the RCAF. No. 2 Technical Training School was moved to Trenton in November. Borden now fell under the jurisdiction of No. 1 Training Command which had stood up in Toronto on 1 January 1940. One of an eventual four Training Commands administering the BCATP, among its first directives was confirmation that RCAF Station Camp Borden would be the home of No. 1 Service Flying Training School (SFTS), in effect establishing the first BCATP flight training facility. Eventually, there would be another twenty-eight SFTS's scattered throughout the country.

Although there had been some flying instruction taking place in the midst of the construction, the first large influx of students would come in the spring of 1940. Anticipating that the large number of trainees would quickly outpace Borden's capacity, surveyors from the Department of Transport arrived in early 1940 to select land suitable for relief fields. By April two locations had been chosen. The first was located in Sunnidale Township, just west of the village of Edenvale. The "Edenvale Aerodrome" was situated on 662 hectares (1635 acres) of property leased from local owners. It boasted three paved runways complete with lighting to facilitate night landings. The other field, referred to as Alliston Field, had only grass strips and night flying could be undertaken only with the aide of flares and pot lights. The total project cost approximately $400,000.

Aircraft, with which to implement the BCATP, were in short supply. Acquiring aircraft from the United States was difficult as that country was not at war and governed by neutrality laws preventing the sale of war material to a belligerent. The United Kingdom was

Left: A later aerial showing the three paved runways and aircraft activity with Avro Ansons on the field, 25 June 1940. *DND PL-578*

Below: Taken on the same flight as the photo on the previous page, this image looks west over the RCAF Station Borden part of Camp Borden, with the airfield in the middle distance. *DND PL-48*

Watching the 30 September 1940 Wings Parade are left to right: Group Captain A.T.N. Cawley, the Honorable J.A. Ralston & an unidentified government official. *DND PL-2220*

Above: The location of this particular photo, officially captioned as "Student pilots watch manoeuvres before taking off at No. 1 Initial Training School (ITS) Borden 30 Jul 1940" may be disputed, but the fact remains that the student pilots on "Course One"of No. 1 SFTS at Borden came from No. 1 ITS, Toronto (Eglington Hunt Club). Of the forty-seven graduates of the Toronto school, thirty-nine would graduate with their Wings won at Borden on 30 September 1940. Half would then receive a commission while the others advanced to NCO ranks. Rather than be posted overseas, most of the first few Courses to graduate from this SFTS would remain in Canada as BCATP instructors. The aircraft in the background is a Harvard Mk.I, part of a small batch of the early fabric-covered fuselage models taken on strength at Borden in December 1939. *DND PL-1119*

Above left: W/C McGill takes the salute during a pre-BCATP Presentation of Wings Parade at Borden, 21 March 1940. The aircraft behind him is a Fairey Battle Bombing & Gunnery trainer. *DND PL-29*

to have provided a certain number of aircraft, but after the successful German invasion of France in the spring of 1940, all British production was dedicated to their immediate needs. Canada's aviation industry, which was just starting to ramp up, could not make up the difference. Therefore, it was a "mixed bag" of aircraft, including civilian types such as the Stinson 105 and Beechcraft 18 and obsolete military machines such as the Nomad and Battle, which greeted students upon their arrival at No. 1 SFTS. Eventually, the North American Harvard would become the most prolific training aircraft at Borden, with the Avro Anson as the dominant twin.

The first intake of BCATP students, appropriately known as "Class One," arrived at Borden on 22 July 1940. Undoubtedly they were overwhelmed by the hectic pace of activity at Borden. Initial construction had focused on flight training facilities, now the emphasis shifted to ensure that all of the support requirements were met. Even as the students attended classroom lectures, logged many hours of Link flight simulator training and mastered the art of safely operating an aircraft, they had to contend with a virtual city being erected around them. By the end of the year, RCAF Camp Borden boasted new supply, maintenance, repair and inspection shops ded-

icated to keeping the aircraft in the air despite what "dents" the student might have inflicted upon them. Additional buildings housed sections dealing with mechanical transport, parachute rigging, meteorology, stores and accounting. Of course there was a ubiquitous parade square. As well, there were sport and recreational facilities for use during free time, not that the students had a lot of that available to them.

In approximately 12 weeks, the first BCATP class of pilots graduated. They were preceded by the sixth and last Provisional Pilot Officer course whose members received their wings on 6 September 1940. Most of the graduates from both groups were recycled back into the BCATP as instructors. There were never enough instructors.

Despite wistful rumours that training would shift from Borden to Florida during the winter months, it was business as usual during the harsh winter of 1940-1941. The westerly orientation of the runway, combined with strong winds, would result in the build-up of massive snow drifts around the hangars and ramps areas. Despite the provision of extra snowploughs, keeping the flying operation moving at a semi-regular pace was a challenge. Still, on 17 March 1941 the members of Class 16 received their wings. Included in its ranks were a number of students from New Zealand, Australia and the United States who probably wished they were back home where it was warm.

text continued on page 50

A panoramic view of the Presentation of Wings Parade attended by W/C McGill at Borden on 21 March 1940. The aircraft in the background are all ex Royal Air Force — two Fairey Battles and a twin-engined Oxford. The Oxford most probably belongs to the RCAF Instructors Training School, a Borden lodger unit at the time. *DND PL-36*

Governor-General Athlone appears to be enjoying his "ride" in the Link Trainer at Borden. *DND PL-2153*

RCAF Station Borden at work and play…

Clockwise from the left:

The library was used fro both pleasure and study.

Students in a class at the Armament School, RCAF Station Borden, 26 June 1940.

Above: A meteorologist at work in the "Met" Room.

Students in a shop class with attentive instructors at the ready.

Left: A group photo of officers in the mess at Borden.

Right: Airman enjoying the recreation facility's billiards tables.

Below: F/O J. Woolfenden and P/O I.M.S. Brown check watches before a Harvard Mk.II flight on 31 July 1940.

Below left: An Australian trainee enjoying a lunch break.

Below right: 29 January 1941, Two Australian trainees enjoy the fresh air and try their hand at skiing at Camp Borden.

DND PL-1090

DND PL-1091

DND PL-1191

Above: Sergeant J.R. Kingsborough in the control tower signaling aircraft with a Very pistol. Above right: Leading Aircraftman C.F.K. Mews sending a message with an Aldis lamp. Right: F/O W.V. Mudray and Sgt R. Hammill prepare for take off in a Harvard Mk.I.
All of these photographs were taken on 30-31 July 1940.

A trainer-yellow Fairey Battle passes the control tower on finals to Runway 29 while a Harvard Mk.I trundles down the taxiway in front of hangar row, 30 July, 1940.

DND PL-1104

Chocks away! An all bare-metal Yale heads out on another sortie. The Yale, with its non-retracting undercarriage was otherwise very similar ot the Harvard.

DND PL-2222

Harvard Mk.I Nos. 1321 and 1343 preparing to leave on a training sortie on 21 March 1940.

DND PL-43

On the same day, a powered-up turret-equipped Anson kicks up its own mini snow squall.

DND PL-51

The War Years: 1939 - 1945   Camp Borden   **48**

RCAF Station Borden MT support...

DND CB-92

LAC PA-052195

Above left: Ford halftrack crash tender. RCAF No. 340 at Borden, on 28 September 1939.

Above: Personnel with a fire engine in front of the RCAF Station's fire hall in October 1944.

A Walter four wheel drive, with a North Star snow loader installed, in action on 21 March 1940.

Below: Ford runabout truck No. 52, 23 August 1939.

DND CB-1909

DND CB-10

In July 1941, No. 1 Training Command decided that the First World War vintage hangars were unsuitable for larger, multi-engine aircraft. Henceforth, No. 1 SFTS would focus on single-engine advanced training utilizing Harvard and Yale aircraft. The training syllabus also placed additional focus on bombing and air firing. Up until this point, this type of training had been conducted in the confines of Camp Borden, but growing army presence made range coordination a major problem. A temporary solution was found with the leasing of land approximately 24 kilometers (15 miles) northwest of the airfield between Lowell and Staynor. However, by July 1942 air-to-ground training was conducted within the confines of the newly acquired Camp Meaford.

The year 1942 also saw the arrival of the first RCAF (Women's Division) members to the station. The Air Women, or "WDs" as they were popularly known, arrived from No. 6 Manning Depot in Toronto and were initially assigned clerical and office duties. They helped swell RCAF ranks to over 1,500 all ranks at Camp Borden. This increase in overall strength was fortunate as the BCATP training syllabus was about to change.

In May 1942, partly to avoid congestion at training establishments in England due to the large volume of graduates, SFTS training was lengthened. Pilots would graduate after a 16 week course with the last four weeks dedicated to advanced training. Combined with an increase in the intake of students, this meant that instructional staff and aircraft resources would also be increased. By the end of the summer, there were 116 aircraft, mostly Harvards and Yales, at Borden.

Training continued at a hectic pace throughout the remainder of 1942 and into 1943. Borden was working at peak efficiency as recognized by several commendations from Ottawa. Much of the credit went to the instructors, but there were never enough of them. Each seasoned pilot was allocated four students to shepherd through

Below left: Leading Air Woman M.A. Ferguson of the Motor Transport Section washes down a gas tender.

Airwomen at work at No. I SFTS, RCAF Station Borden on 18 August 1942. The original caption notes that "the Women's Division of the RCAF do a man-sized job in helping to keep things running smoothly. Here two of them expertly handle the tricky job of gathering the shrouds, a very important phase of parachute packing."

DND PL-9853

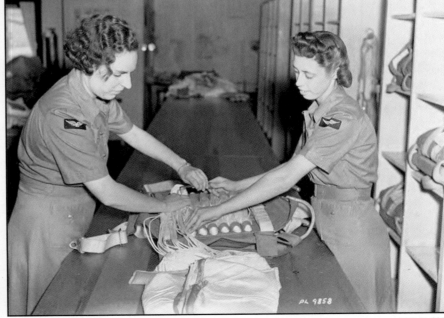

DND PL-9858

Above: Twelve turret-equipped Ansons — two of them still in camouflage finish — over a typically pastoral southwestern Ontario countryside, 25 June 1940. *DND PL-581*

Above right: LAC Stanislas Bernier of Levis, Quebec, appears to be a jovial sort of student pilot in amongst the many yellow and bare metal Harvards in this 23 April 1941 No. 1 SFTS photo. *DND PL-3382*

flight training. Their reward – two weeks leave after every 24 weeks of training. And towards the end of 1943 and the beginning of 1944, the training that they were responsible for now included an increased emphasis on low-level flying, reflecting the needs of the air forces in Europe.

Although the bulk of the trainees that went through Borden were Canadian, there were also students present from most of the Commonwealth countries, as well as allied nations such as France and Belgium. Americans, up until the United States entered the war in December 1941, made up the single largest national contingent even though they served as members of the RCAF. In November 1944, Course No. 93, saw the presentation of pilot wings to members of the Royal Norwegian Air Force. Members of this service had been training in Canada since 1940 after their country had been occupied by Germany.

Although bitter fighting in Europe and the Far East continued

into 1945, the need for additional aircrew was declining rapidly. Air Force recruiting had been on the decline since the previous summer and the closure or amalgamation of BCATP schools was accelerated. This meant an increase in students and aircraft for Borden. Meanwhile, Its SFTS course was lengthened to twenty weeks. On 29 March 1945, the last BCATP course graduated at RCAF Station Camp Borden with over 100 members of the RCAF and Commonwealth air forces receiving their wings.

During its 56 month association with the BCATP, No. 1 SFTS, RCAF Station Camp Borden, had graduated 2,728 Commonwealth pilots of which 1790 were Canadian. Over the next two months more and more RCAF personnel departed the station which quickly took on a "quietness" reminiscent of its pre-war days. Although it had been determined that Borden would continue to operate as an aircraft maintenance and repair centre, its future was far from certain.

The final Wings Parade, for Courses 121 and 122 of No. 1 SFTS at RCAF Station Borden on 29 March 1945, with plenty of dignitaries, brass, graduates, and aircraft in attendance. *DND CB-3427-2*

Inset photo: The proudest moment in any young military pilots' life — the presentation of wings by a senior officer. LAC W.A. Elliott of 1566 Dougall Avenue, Windsor, Ontario, was among the graduates receiving their RCAF pilot's wings in a ceremony at No. 1 SFTS, RCAF Station Borden on Thursday, 1 April 1943. In the above, LAC Elliott is shown receiving his wings from Air Commodore F.S. McGill, Air Officer Commanding No. 1 Training Command, who officiated at the graduation. McGill had been the first CO of the School here in 1940. *DND PL-16357*

Members of the Royal Canadian Armoured Corps (RCAC) holding a Corps weekend at Camp Borden in the mid 1960's. On this occasion, they also commemorated the 50th Anniversary of the outbreak of the First World War. Maj Gen F.F. Worthington, Honorary Colonel Commandant of the Corps, takes the salute during the march past of men and the roll past of Centurion tanks at the RCAC School.

DND Z-10381-1

A Transition to Peacetime… Again

The years 1946 and 1947 were ones of transition for the RCAF as it moved to a peace-time footing. Tens of thousands of personnel had to be eased back into civilian life as the air force went from a wartime high of over 250,000 to an effective post-war strength of 12,000. Thousands of aircraft, both BCATP trainers and operational service machines, were disposed of. Facilities across the country were either mothballed or abandoned.

There was never serious consideration given to closing RCAF Station Borden. As one of two primary pre-war RCAF stations it was culturally ingrained in the psyche of most senior air officers as a training establishment. However, more powerful aircraft and the emergence of jet technology meant that Borden's future as a flying training centre was questionable without substantial upgrades. Reductions in defence spending rendered the point moot and on 31 March 1946, No. 1 Service Flying Training School closed. At the same time No. 2 Technical Training School (TTS), re-located back to Borden from its war-time location in St. Thomas, Ontario. With the stand-up of this unit on 1 April, Borden resumed its previous role as the "technical schoolhouse" for the RCAF.

Until the early 1950's, maximum use was made of the existing buildings and infrastructure to meet the modest training demands of a small air force. This all changed with the advent of the Cold War and Canadian participation in defensive alliances such as the North Atlantic Treaty Organization (NATO) and, in 1957, North American Aerospace Defence Command (NORAD). An unprecedented peace-time increase in the Canadian Forces in general, and the RCAF in particular, coupled with the acquisition of new aircraft such as the Canadair Sabre and Avro CF-100 Canuck fighters, resulted in a new period of expansion for RCAF Station Borden.

The growing number of aviation technical students quickly outpaced the ability to provide the necessary training using the war-time vintage facilities. In 1952 construction began on a brand-new building that would become the new home for No. 2 TTS and the centre for technical training in the RCAF. Occupied in 1953, Croil Hall soon began to "hum" as instructors imparted to a new genera-

tion of airmen and airwomen the knowledge and skills required for the jet age. Two new hangars were built soon after to house static training aircraft and equipment that could not be accommodated in Croil Hall. Also accommodated in these hangars was a small Station Flight, equipped primarily with the Beech 18 Expeditor aircraft, for utility and training support as required.

With an eye to the future construction began on a brand-new training building in 1958. Christened the Stedman Building, it would house state-of-the-art avionics and technical training facilities to support Canada's proposed new fighter, the CF-105 Avro Arrow. Unfortunately, this was not to be as the Arrow programme was

Technicians working on the landing gear of a Harvard aircraft. With the closing of the wartime No. 1 SFTS, No. 2 TTS moved from RCAF Station St. Thomas, Ontario, back to Borden, the technical schoolhouse of the Air Force.

DND PL-52341

An interior view of the No. 2 TTS facility constructed at RCAF Station Borden since 1950. Here, the forward and rear fuselage sections of Canadair-built Sabre airframes are mounted on work stands for the purpose of technical instruction. *DND PL-56410*

Below: A DHC-1 Chipmunk trainer in basic mid 1950's markings.

Below right: A Beechcraft Expeditor Mk. 3 with the short-lived late 1940's era RCAF markings.

These would become the last military aircraft types to operate out of Borden while it was still an RCAF Station.

cancelled in 1959. By that time, the Stedman Building had been completed and all the necessary training equipment purchased and installed. Although the Stedman Building would remain as part of No. 2 TTS, upon receiving news of the project's demise orders were given to strip the building of most of the Arrow-specific material.

A new decade brought with it new aircraft and new training responsibilities. There were now 88 different trades, ranging from avionics technician to laundry operator in the peace-time RCAF, most of which were taught at Borden. Under the auspices of Training Command, No. 2 TTS was disbanded to be replaced, by 1964, with seven different schools: Airborne Electronic Training, Fire Fighter, Support Services, Air Traffic Control, Supervisor Services Training, Technical Services and Aircraft Trades. The courses they offered ranged from a few weeks to almost a full twelve months with approximately 3000 students graduated each year.

Flight training returned to Borden, albeit briefly, in 1966 with the closure of RCAF Station Centralia, Ontario. One hundred and twenty personnel from the Primary Flying School (PFS), along with

their CT-120 Chipmunk aircraft, arrived in September and quickly set-up shop utilizing both the new and old hangars. For approximately the next four years, the PFS would provide basic flight training to would-be pilots for the Canadian Army, Royal Canadian Navy, RCAF and a number of foreign students. This integrated approach to flight training was a sign of things to come. In Borden, the upcoming integration of the military services would result in massive changes to both the RCAF's and Canadian Army's approach to training. *text continued on page 59*

DND PC-1069

DND RE-4730-2

DND PL-39335

DND PL-87508

DND PL-39341

Clockwise, from the left:

The RCAF No. 2 TTS had some of the finest wood working equipment for the repair of both aircraft and station facilities.

Former aircrew members of the RCAF who had graduated from Canadian universities became Technical Officers. Here, trainees F/L D.B. Wurtele and F/L K.R. Grimley examine a Goblin jet engine from a Vampire fighter.

AC2 James R. MacKenzie is installing a pitot head in the air intake of an F-86 Sabre.

Sgt. W.E.T. Harwood uses a synthetic cockpit trainer to demonstrate to LAC P.J. Wirt how a Sperry automatic pilot actually works in flight.

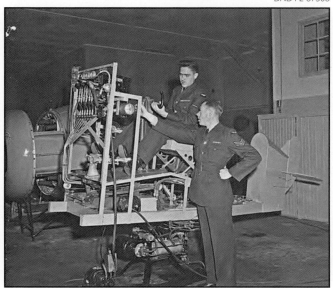

DND PL-39345

DND PCN-7001

DND CB69-1917

Above: A little inspiration for aspiration... the Golden Hawks aerial demonstration team execute a five-aircraft low pass, trailing red and blue smoke from their Sabres on Air Force Day, 1962, at Camp Borden.

Above left: Chipmunk 18076 at Camp Borden in late 1960's transitional markings — even as the post-unification era heralded in a new Canadian Forces markings scheme, RCAF titles persisted for a time on some aircraft.

Exterior view of the new Technical Training School building, Croil Hall, constructed at Borden in the 1953.

DND PL-56409D

Above: An oblique aerial view of the new Technical Training School building, revealing its enclosed central square. The baseball diamond left of frame gives a good impression of scale. The two hangars in the background are new postwar structures as well. These are at the northeast end of the old First World War era "hangar row" of wooden hangars — some (out of an original fifteen) of which are still standing. A Lancaster parked on the hardstand beyond also gives an impression of the size of these new hangars. *DND PL-130183*

A restored Second World War era Spitfire sits in as "gate guard" to the Administration Building at RCAF Station Borden. Note the Air Force Ensign flying from the flagpole.

DND PL-130183

The Avro CF-105 Arrow

Designed in the 1950's to meet Canada's requirement for a high-speed, high-altitude interceptor, the delta-winged CF-105 Arrow was built by A.V. Roe Canada at its plant in Malton, Ontario. Intended to be employed against manned-bombers, the first aircraft, RL-201, had the misfortune to roll-out on 4 October 1957, the same day that the Soviet Union launched Sputnik 1 into space. Over the next several years, the Arrow would go through a series of design modifications and flight testing. However, rising productions costs coupled with a weakening Canadian economy resulted in the controversial cancellation of the project on 20 February 1959. A total of five Arrows had been completed, with a sixth nearly finished, prior to the termination of the programme.

The Royal Canadian Air Force anticipated that the CF-105 would serve Canada for decades. Therefore, hundreds of thousands of dollars were spent at RCAF Station Camp Borden for new buildings, training facilities and instructional equipment to support this state-of-the-art aircraft. With the cancellation of the programme much of the Arrow-specific equipment was removed and disposed of, but the buildings and facilities remained with the air force training family and continue to be utilized today.

...And on the Other Side of the Camp

Much like the RCAF, the Canadian Army spent the years immediately following the end of the Second World War in a state of flux as the nation, and the service, adjusted to peace. For much of this period, Camp Borden was utilized as a transitional facility for personnel returning from overseas. Approximately 60 percent of the buildings at Borden were envisaged as temporary and where possible they were either dismantled or mothballed. A much smaller permanent staff utilized only a fraction of the remaining buildings and although there was some discussion with respect to the possibility of closing the Camp, it came to naught.

By 1946, the Canadian government had settled on a peacetime army strength of 25,000 supported by a substantial reserve component. In February of that year, Ottawa announced that Borden would remain open as a land training centre and would continue to provide armoured, medical, service and support training. On 1 April 1946, the Canadian School of Infantry was established at Borden and for the first time all phases of infantry training would be consolidated at one place. Soon thereafter, the Camp was placed under the overall command of the General Officer Command, Central Command, with a Commandant not to exceed the rank of Colonel.

For the next three years the various army schools sorted themselves out. Although they continued to provide some training, their efforts were more focused on downsizing and adapting existing facilities. Camp Meaford continued to be utilized for armour and artillery training. Then the advent of the Cold War, and Canada's commitment to providing a brigade to both Europe and Korea, led to a massive increase in Canada's army.

At first the influx of trainees was accommodated utilizing the existing infrastructure. However, throughout the 1950's and 1960's accommodations, messing and training facilities were gradually replaced with newer, permanent structures. Ranges were upgraded as well reflecting changing doctrine, equipment and technology. Nuclear, biological and chemical training was emphasized, as was the

text continued on page 63

North Korea invaded South Korea on 25 June 1950 and, as part of a United Nations (UN) response, Canada authorized the formation of a Canadian Army Special Service Force to serve under UN command. Although raised and trained as part of the regular Army, the Force was filled with individuals, many of them veterans of the Second World War, enrolled for a period of 18 months (or longer under certain conditions). The units of what would become the 25th Canadian Infantry Brigade Group were established as separate parts of existing Active Force regiments. Where necessary, members of the Active Force would "flesh out" the Force units.

Under the initial command of Brigadier General J.M. Rockingham, the original units of the Brigade Group consisted of the second battalions of the Royal Canadian Regiment, Princess Patricia's Canadian Light Infantry, and the Royal 22e Régiment; "C" Squadron of the Lord Stratchona's Horse; 2nd Field Regiment, Royal Canadian Horse Artillery; 57th Canadian Independent Field Squadron, Royal Canadian Engineers; 25th Infantry Brigade Group Signal Squadron, No. 54 Canadian Transport Company, Royal Canadian Army Service Corps; and No. 25 Field Ambulance, Royal Canadian Army Medical Corps. Five hundred and sixteen Canadians died in the conflict.

Many of the members of the Canadian Army Special Service Force trained, either specifically for Korea or during the Second World War, at Camp Borden.

Canadian Rocks in Korea — In this picture are Brig Gen Rockingham, Cpl Rocky Prentice, and Pte Rocky Laroque.

DND SF-4257

Top: PPCLI snipers in Korea.   DND SF-6067

Above: Left to right, Ptes A.F. Proulx and J.M. Aubin of the Royal 22e Regiment at a front-line position with grenades at the ready, December 1952.   DND SF-5699

The 2nd Battalion Princess Patricia's Canadian Light Infantry in the combat area, Korea, 23 April 1951.

DND SF-1362

Camp Borden, a mid 1960's Aerial Perspective

DND RE75-384

DND RE75-382

DND RE75-377

DND RE75-374

Far right: A two man team of the Reconnaissance and Monitoring Platoon of The Black Watch enter a highly radioactive "hot spot" during exercise "Trial Run" the last of three exercises conducted by Regular Army Units at Camp Borden on civil defence. At right Lt. Wes Hawkins, team leader, measures the concentration of radioactivity in the "hot spot". His assistant, Sgt. Ernest Class, at left, notes down the degree of concentration and reports the figure to his HQ, using a No. 510 wireless set strapped to his back. More than 250 regular Army soldiers took part in the realistic exercise on 27 April 1959.

DND CC-11881

ability to survive and fight on a nuclear battlefield. The training was to be provided to both the Regular and Reserve force, but in the early 1960's the Canadian Militia were re-oriented towards civil defence deceasing the amount of training they were provided at Borden. Still, virtually all of the regular force personnel that served in Europe, and many of those who served in Korea, spent time at Camp Borden.

In the late 1950's, the threat of a possible nuclear war was such that both federal and provincial governments constructed underground bunkers. Camp Borden was chosen to house Ontario's emergency government shelter and the "secret" facility was constructed over the next few years. A second, smaller communications bunker was built on the site of the old BCATP relief airfield at Elmdale. Although the bunkers were used for a variety of other purposes throughout their existence they were fortunately never called upon to fulfill their primary purpose.

In 1965, the Combat Arms School was established amalgamating basic land-oriented training that had been provided by both the Royal Canadian School of Infantry and the Royal Canadian Armoured Corps School. Joining these organizations in the mid-1960's were other training units such as School of Military Intelligence, Royal Canadian Army Service Corps School, the Canadian Provost Corps School and the Army Physical Training Centre. The thousands of trainees accommodated each year meant a large permanent staff. When combined with the full-time presence of the RCAF, this meant that Station / Camp community went through some major changes.

text continued on page 67

Below: Four RCN(R) officers learning to use a radio device that simulates dangerous doses of radioactivity at the ABCD School. Left to right: Cdr K. Glashen; Lt J.G. Ashton; WO W. MacLean, instructor, Lt. T.C. Cross, and LCdr G. Ballard.   *DND COND-5853*

Loading some of the seventy-six Battalion jeeps near Camp Borden during exercise *Nomad*. The 2ⁿᵈ Battalion, the Royal Canadian Regiment, was the only infantry unit then equipped solely with these vehicles which can be readily transported by air.   *DND CC-10259*

London Militia members at Camp: Signalman Jim Bennett, left, and Corporal Martin McGrenere check a convoy route on the map of Camp Borden during a training exercise while attending the annual summer camp attachment of their unit, No. 9 Signals Regiment (Militia), London, to No. 2 Signals Squadron, Royal Canadian Signals (Regular).   *DND CC-12291-14*

An early-mid 1960's demonstration at Borden with the then-new de Havilland Canada DHC-7 Caribou short take-off and landing transport aircraft. Sharp-eyed viewers will notice the US Army presence at this event. After some modification to production standard, this particular Caribou (the second prototype) would go on to a career with the mysterious Air America (the CIA's "air arm" in Southeast Asia), while the regular US military also operated the type "in country" during the Vietnam War. Caribou No. 2 is presently on display in the Yankee Air Museum.   *DND CC-11019*

Training, training, & more training

Infantrymen charging during training at Camp Borden, circa 1967.

DND CF67-438-3

Bazookas in the RCAF! Army Cpl E. "Emilien" Lacroix, right, watches carefully as LAC E.O. "Ed" Deisting, left, feeds a round into the launcher, while LAC R. "Dick" Dow holds the gun in firing position, during rocket firing practice. The LACs were members of the first RCAF Ground Defence Course and on completion of the training were sent out as instructors to other RCAF Stations.

DND CF67-438-3

CB2007-0194-13

Left: Canadian Army trucks during a halt on exercise at Camp Borden.

Right: Watermanship training — ROTP students try out a temporary foot bridge they have built at Camp Borden.

CDN63-81-3

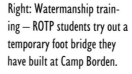

DND CF67-1000-62

Left: A Sherman tank plays the "enemy" role, waiting in cover for cadets during a training exercise on the Meaford Range.

DND CF67-438-5

Right: An Infantry mortar section training at Borden with the 81 mm mortar and an M113 armoured vehicle.

Right: Officer cadets at RCAC School prepare ammunition for loading into Centurion tank at Meaford Tank Range, 3 Aug 1967.

DND CF67-1000-70

DND CF67-438-1

Left: An Infantry Section Commander explains relative positions to his men during an exercise.

The Borden Community

The post-war RCAF, and the Canadian Army, now had to deal with a growing number of dependents as more and more of its personnel started families. At first excess accommodation buildings were hastily remodeled into temporary housing for families, but beginning in 1949, and carrying on for almost a decade, permanent married quarters (PMQs) were erected at Borden. Eventually there would be a total of 1029 PMQs built at Borden and nearby locations such as Camp Meaford.

The growing number of children made it impractical to continue to bus them to schools located in surrounding communities so between 1952 and 1957 four public schools were built: one for the RCAF and three for the Canadian Army. Prior to the end of the decade the lower schools would be joined by the Camp Borden District High School (grades nine to 13). Two boards, the Camp Borden District High School Board and the Camp Borden Public School Board, administered the schools under the auspices of the Ontario Department of Education. RCAF dependents attended the high school and one air force member sat on the board.

Various amenities were shared by all personnel at Borden. For the most part they were administered by Maple Leaf Services. They included a grocery store, service station, bowling alley, six wet and

New recruits arriving by train.

CB2007-0194-078

four dry canteens, four snack bars, dry cleaning and a shoe-repair shop. It was estimated that these enterprises grossed over $1 million annually. The Camp Borden Citizen, the local newspaper, boasted a weekly circulation of over 1600. There was an indoor and outdoor pool, ice arena, public library, and dog pound. The theatre was extremely popular with shows seven days a week and matinees on Saturday and Sunday.

In addition to the various army, air and sea cadet units, numerous youth organizations were established. Boy Scouts, Girl Guides and Brownies were joined by a thriving Teen Town. At one point there sixteen little league teams and as many as 11 hockey teams for boys. Nor where the adults neglected and those who wished could participate in clubs such as golf, curling, drama, art, and flying to name but a few.

By the mid-1960's Borden as a whole was as big, if not bigger, than some of the nearby communities. It was administered by "mayors" for both the RCAF and Army portions of the Camp supported by a community council and responsible to their respective chains of command. However, the dual communities, much like individual approach to service training was about to undergo a massive change due to government directed unification of the armed forces.

text continued on page 72

DND PL-56384-D

DND PL-52354

Above: An eight-room on-base school.

Left: The new Central Heating Plant constructed after 1949.

Right: This Esso gas station was new to the Camp in the 1950's.

View of PMQs looking from house No. 1 to house No. 18 adjacent to No. 13 "X" Depot at Camp Borden. *DND PL-52228*

Domestic area buildings including the combined mess, combined lounge, barracks and PMQs near the pump house and water reservoir near No. 13 "X" Depot at Camp Borden. *DND PL-52231*

Shopping at the Maple Leaf Services Store on base in the 1950's.

Growth – as seen from above

The official caption for this high-altitude vertical photograph includes a reference to March 1964. However, Croil Hall has yet to be constructed, so it was most certainly taken sometime between 1945 and 1953.

DND RE-75-460

A closer up aerial of the airfield portion of RCAF Station Borden taken at the same time as the photograph on page 69. *DND RE-75-461*

A later high-altitude vertical aerial photograph taken of the overall Camp Borden complex from 10,550 feet (3200 metres), date-stamped 24 April 1965. Note the presence of the two new hangars and their hardstands, behind them Croil Hall, and the distinctive oval race track adjacent to these new additions to the airfield side of the Camp. *DND RE-70-1757*

Maj Gen F.F. Worthington, Honorary Colonel Commandant of the Corps and his First World War driver "Pop" Saunders look over bullet holes in the machine gun armed armoured fighting vehicle they'd used in combat. The antique was loaned to the school by the War Museum for this 50th Anniversary event. "Fighting" Frank" as he was called by men in the First and Second World Wars will take the salute during the march past of men and the roll past of tanks at the RCAC School (see pg. 53).

DND Z-10381-1

Maj Gen Worthington takes the salute riding in the antique First World War vintage armoured car at Borden during the Cadet Parade on 14 August 1966. The other officers in the vehicle are Col Greenleaf, Commandant / Director of Armour, and Lt Geddrey, Aide De Camp to the Colonel Commandant.

DND CB66-370-1

The Borden side of the funeral procession for General F. F. Worthington, who died at Ottawa's Military Hospital on 8 December 1967. After his funeral in Ottawa, his casket was flown to Borden by an RCAF Caribou transport aircraft. In accordance with his wishes, his remains were interred in the Camp's Worthington Park. In his honour, four RCAC Centurion tanks fired a thirteen gun salute and three RCAF Chipmunk aircraft did a low-level flypast.

DND CB67-682-1

Unification

Under Minister of National Defence Paul Hellyer, the 1964 Defence White Paper outlined a major reorganization of the Canadian Forces whereby the three services would be unified into a single entity under a functional command system. To this effect, Bill C-243, The Canadian Forces Reorganization Act received Royal Assent on 1 February 1968. As of that date, the Royal Canadian Navy, Canadian Army and RCAF ceased to exist as they became, collectively, the Canadian Armed Forces, or Canadian Forces (CF). However, Canadian Forces Base (CFB) Borden had already stood up a year earlier.

Although not universally welcomed by the members of the various services, unification came as no surprise. For several years prior to the passing of Bill C-243, exactly how Borden would be reorganized was being discussed. Regardless of how the re-structuring would proceed, no one doubted that it would be a massive undertaking. As of January 1967, Borden was one of the largest training bases in the country occupying almost 50 square kilometers (31 square miles) of territory connected by over 111 kilometers (69 miles) of roads. Between them, the RCAF and Canadian Army were

responsible for 57 buildings built prior to 1938, 366 more erected during the Second World War and a further 133 post-war structures that could be considered "modern." With an annual maintenance budget in excess of $2 million dollars, one of the first areas to complete its reorganization was Construction Engineering (CE) as its personnel was responsible for the upkeep of the infrastructure. Having begun in December 1966, the amalgamation of the 24 Works Company, Royal Canadian Engineers, and the RCAF's CE Section was completed by March 1967.

In a letter to the Canadian Forces Comptroller, Air Vice Marshal R.C. Stovel, the commander, Canadian Forces Training Command, outlined some of the issues to be dealt with under unification as Borden adapted to changing roles and a new organizational posture. There were 16 schools at Borden of which two, the Royal Canadian Army Service Corps School and the Combat Arms School, were commanded by Colonels. Under unification the newly designated Canadian Forces Bases would be commanded by Colonels; however, given the scope of its responsibilities and the size of some of the schools, Borden should be commanded by a Brigadier-General who would be responsible for coordination of all training. A "base-commander" at the Colonel level would handle the day-to-day administration of the base.

Hangar No. 1 of the fifteen First World War era Hangars, photographed sometime after 1950, stands as a prime example of the original-construction infrastructure still in use (albeit, some of it repurposed) throughout the postwar expansion years leading up to unification. *DND PL-56377-A*

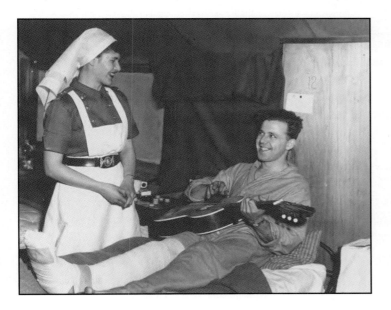

Left: Purple trades — an injured soldier playing guitar to a nurse in the pre-unification Camp Borden days. For Disciplines such as nursing, unification would have little real effect on the actual workday, but a profound effect on administration, CF bookkeeping, and Department of National Defence "big picture" organizational charts. *CB2007-0194-06*

Elevating overall control of CFB Borden to a general officer was deemed necessary not only because of the importance of all of the "air element" technical and trades training. For the "land element" the individual would be responsible to meet the post-recruit, specialist and continuation training for officers and non-commissioned members of the armoured, artillery and infantry. With this in mind, it was recommended that the general officer always have a combat arms background.

Stovel also recommended that six of the seven smaller former-RCAF schools be amalgamated into one large CF Aircraft Trades School. He also suggested that the Combat Arms School absorb the Canadian School of Military Intelligence. Finally, he advocated the combining of the Royal Canadian Army Service Corps School, Canadian Provost Corps School, CF Nuclear, Biological and Chemical Warfare School, Army Physical Training Centre and RCAF Support Services School into one large Combat and Administrative Support Services School.

Most of these recommendations never came to pass. By 1970, CFB Borden was under the command of Brigadier-General G.C. Edwards a former naval commodore. Under his direct supervision were the following schools: CF School of Administration and Logistics, CF School of Aerospace and Ordnance Engineering, CF Medical Services School, CF Dental School, CF School of Intelligence and Security, CF Nuclear, Biological and Chemical Warfare School, CF

Architect of Canadian Armed Forces unification, Mr. Paul T. Hellyer (centre), Minister of National Defence of Canada, is seen here arriving at Gaza airport to pay a one-day visit to the Canadian Troops serving with the United Nations Emergency Force (UNEF). He is being escorted by Major-General Carlos Flores Paiva Chaves (left), UNEF Commander, and Colonel D.H. Rochester, Commander of the Canadian contingent.

UN News & Media photo 142575

School of Physical Education and Recreation and the CF School of Instruction Technique. In addition, there were 11 lodger units supported by Borden.

The changes at Borden were not limited to the combining of former service training establishments. In January 1970, the last Expeditor aircraft departed the base bringing to an end Borden's existence as a flying station. Little more than a month later, the Primary Flight School was shifted to CFB Portage la Prairie, Manitoba. Its 27 Chipmunk aircraft were transported to their new location via CC-130 Hercules with the last flight out taking place on 4 May. With this unit's departure the airfield was place on uncontrolled Visual Flight Rules (VFR) status with only minimal ability to support transiting aircraft.

Major changes were afoot as well with respect to land forces training. In June, the Combat Arms School was transferred to CFB Gagetown, New Brunswick. For all practicable purposes the move was completed that summer and what equipment that remained behind, such as a number of Centurion tanks, were either mothballed or placed at the disposal of training establishments.

Even with the departure of these major schools, CFB Borden remained one of the largest bases in Canada. Over 2700 military personnel were living in PMQs or single quarters with an additional 626 living in nearby civilian communities. They were supported in their duties by over 1390 civilian employees. The local community continued to be robust with almost 5000 dependents living within the confines of the base and approximately 1750 students went to school at Borden.

As the base entered a new decade, and more and more CF personnel sported "rifle green" uniforms, Borden's new badge was proudly on display. Approved in June 1968, reflecting the new CF heraldic requirements, a queen's crown symbolizing the relationship of the CF to the Sovereign is atop a wreath of maple leaves indicative of Canada. A green pine tree, the central device of the former Canadian Army Camp, was retained and centred within a green circle over the name "Borden." Completing the badge is the motto of RCAF Station Borden, *E Principio*, "From the Very Beginning." With two distinct heritage paths, CFB Borden had embarked on a new era.

The 1964 Defence White paper proposed a major reorganization of the military forces of Canada. The Canadian Army, Royal Canadian Navy (RCN) and Royal Canadian Air Force (RCAF) would cease to be separate services and become a single unified force under a functional command system. Despite opposition for certain senior officers and veteran's groups, on 1 February 1968, Bill C-242, the Canadian Forces Reorganization Act was given Royal Assent and the Canadian Forces came into being.

Air staff at RCAF Station Camp Borden and Army staff at Camp Borden were already working on the necessary procedures and processes required to establish Canadian Forces Base (CFB) Borden. As a result, although there were challenges to be overcome, the transition to the new organizational construct proceed relatively smoothly. Service-specific schools were replaced by new Canadian Forces entities while air and land base support functions were amalgamated. Perhaps the most noticeable changes was a mild confusion as all ranks adjusted to new titles, changes in the chain of command and the introduction of new "rifle-green" uniforms.

In August 2011, the historical service names were re-introduced to the three environmental elements of the Canadian Armed Forces. Although the RCAF, RCN and Canadian Army are now once again part of Canada's military lexicon, the overall impact on CFB Borden has been minimal. As it was in 1916, and continuing to this very day, Borden remains focused on training professional, dedicated military personnel to serve Canada as required.

Canadian Forces DHC-3 Otter No. 3671 receives the attention of a "squad" technicians during the instalation and inspection of amphibious floats. All CF Aerospace technical tradespeople receive training at CFB Borden.

October Crisis, 1970

In the fall of 1970, CFB Borden was adjusting to the transfer of major land and air training establishments to other bases. At the same time reorganization of the remaining schools, as well as Borden's internal structure, in accordance with unified guidelines was continuing apace. However, the focus on these mundane tasks was shattered during the first two weeks of October when actions by the Front de Libération du Québec (FLQ) resulted in the Federal government implementing sections of the War Measures Act. The October Crisis had begun.

Borden became involved in the crisis at 1000 hours on 18 October when the Commandant of the CF Security and Intelligence School (CFSIS) was tasked directly to provide military police and intelligence personnel support to what would become Operations GINGER and ESSAY. Over a three-day period 55 personnel were dispatched to various locations utilizing Otter and Buffalo aircraft. At the same time, the base implemented a heightened security posture and called out the Base Defence Force. Armed guards were posted at sensitive points and access to the base was restricted.

The bulk of the support requirements during the crisis fell upon Borden's Base Transportation Section. Large quantities of ammunition and riot control equipment were transported via truck-convoy from Borden and the vicinity to various bases, such as Ottawa and Petawawa, that were serving as staging locations for other units. Often called out at a moment's notice, the transportation section got little rest over the next few weeks. They were even required to provide staff cars and drivers as part of the funeral for Quebec's minister of labour, Pierre Laporte, who had been murdered by the FLQ on 17 October.

By 20 November, the CF operations had come to a close and things returned to normal at Borden and other bases. However, the suddenness of the crisis revealed serious problems in Borden's chain of command that needed to be rectified. Not the least of which was the direct tasking of units and schools on the base without reference to Training Command Headquarters (TCHQ) which was responsible for Borden. All in all, it was a busy end to the first year of the new decade.

Somewhere in Quebec... Land Force vehicles at the ready in the mid-November wake of the October Crisis of 1970. *Duncan Cameron photo via LAC*

A riot control exercise being held by CFSIS, CFB Borden in the early 1970's.
DND CB74-185

Ongoing Reorganization

The release of a new defence White Paper in 1971 led to a reduction in personnel and resources throughout the CF. As Borden struggled to meet its share of the cuts, consolidation and centralization of base resources continued. The downgrading of the airfield was completed with the closure of the tower and radio facilities, transfer of associated technicians and the disposal of equipment. All was not doom and gloom as construction began on a Data Processing Centre that would serve the entire CF. It would take almost two years to complete.

During this period Borden acquired new training responsibilities. A pilot project for Aboriginal and Eskimo students to be trained as aircraft mechanic helpers was initiated in 1971. The following summer a CF English Language Training Unit was stood up and a detachment of the CF Officers Candidate School from Chilliwack, British Columbia, took up residence. For the next few years this detachment would be responsible to train officer cadets that could not be accommodated at Chilliwack.

Two separate events dominated 1972. The first was a rumor that the Toronto International Airport was to be shut down and a new airport opened in Borden. The shear impossibility of such a move taking place did not stop the base, and base commander, from being inundated by telephone calls from the press and concerned citizens. The second event was the rapid change in base commanders. In accordance with a normal posting cycle, Brigadier-General E.M.D. Leslie took command on 22 August, but resigned on 11 September to pursue a political career. He was followed by a succession of acting commanders until Colonel A. H. Middleton was given the node in November.

Over the next four years numerous changes would occur in Borden, some due to ongoing planning and consolidation of training within the CF, others to misadventure. On 4 May 1974, Ottawa announced that over the next three years the CF Medical School would be transferred to Kingston bringing an end to a medical training presence on the base that stretched back to 1946. That same year, the Canadian Forces Junior Leaders School (CFJLS) opened with the first class, consisting of 225 corporals and leading seamen from across Canada, commencing instruction in March. Training establishments in Borden, as well as the rest of the Department of National Defence (DND), came under new management on 1 September 1975 with the re-designation of Training Command to the CF Training System. The new organization was commanded by Brigadier-General L.V. Johnson with its headquarters located at CFB Trenton. Johnson would have under his command CFBs Cornwallis, Nova Scotia, St. Jean, Quebec, Chilliwack, British Columbia, as well as Borden and Kingston in Ontario.

The CFB Borden Headquarters, 1974.

CB2007-0082

The 1960's were a turbulent time in Canadian history. Civic unrest in Quebec lead to a rash of protests and bombings orchestrated by the Front de libération du Québec (FLQ), a group advocating the violent separation of the province from Canada. Two high-profile kidnappings by the FLQ, British diplomat James Cross on 5 October and Quebec Minster of Labour Pierre Laporte on 10 October elevated the level of concern in Ottawa and Quebec City. In response to these actions on 11 October 1970, the Solicitor General of Canada requested support from Mobile Command of the Canadian Forces (CF) to protect sensitive locations in Ottawa and federal property in Quebec, primarily CF facilities housing nuclear weapons. On 12 October approximately 1000 troops were committed to Operation GINGER providing assistance to civil authority.

Three days later the Attorney General of Quebec formally requested federal support. Operation ESSAY commenced almost immediately with the airlift and ground trans-port of thousands of Canadian troops from across Canada. Most would be located in Montreal as part of the aid to civil power mission. Prime Minister Pierre Trudeau's liberal government enacted the War Measures Act on 16 October giving the federal and provincial governments extraordinary powers of search, seizure and arrest. The next day Laporte's body was found in Montreal in the trunk of a car.

Over the next several weeks CF personnel guarded vital points, conducted security patrols in Montreal and aided Quebec police forces in various operations searching for the terrorists. By late December 1970, Laporte's murders had been apprehended and several members of the FLQ exiled to Cuba. Operations GINGER and ESSAY gradually wound down and for all practical purposes were over by February 1971. At its height approximately 12,000 CF air and ground personnel were involved in these operations, including a large supporting contingent from Canadian Forces Base Borden.

CF personnel guarding Iroquois helicopters while in Montreal during the FLQ Crisis.   *DND PCN70-454*

A Voyageur helicopter in flight near a large building during FLQ Crisis in Montreal.   *DND PCN70-468*

A Nomad helicopter leaving La Citadelle and motor transport vehicles of R22R present.   *DND PCN70-468*

A view of the heavy rescue simulated wrecked buildings used for RCAF Fire-fighter Training at Borden.
DND RNC-1226-117

This period of Borden's history also seemed to be somewhat fire-prone. In early 1973, the Canadian Exchange (CANEX) main storage facility was completely destroyed by fire and later that year one of the buildings used to house the officer training detachment went up in flames. The causes of the latter fire never determined. In May of the following year a building housing the Base Non-Technical Workshop and Training Aids Carpenter Shop was also lost to fire. Therefore, it was most apropos when the new Borden Fire Hall was completed in August.

The Base Borden Military Museum annex opened in May 1975 initially housing the collections belonging to the Royal Canadian Army Service Corps and Electrical and Mechanical Engineer museums. Barely 12 months later the Borden Museum Committee was tasked to examine the possibility of including an air force element within the base museum. Eventually it would be housed in one of the original First World War hangers that still existed on the flight line. Reflecting the air force heritage of Borden, work began to refurbish the existing runways.

Recognizing the need to replace and refurbish much of the dated buildings and infrastructure at Borden, CF Training Systems submitted a detailed development plan to Ottawa towards the end of 1976. Although not fully funded, many of the recommendations put forward came to fruition over the next several years. Substandard training accommodation and messing facilities were either replaced or renovated. New staff quarters were erected and, where feasible, student quarters were brought up to modern standards.

The new buildings were needed. Since the beginning of the decade training at Borden had steadily increased. In 1972, as the CAF continued to sort itself out after unification, just less than 8,000 students combined had graduated from all of the schools. By 1979, more than 13,000 trainees graduated from a host of establishments. Under the auspices of the CF Training System Borden hosted the following: CF School of Administration and Logistics, CF Medical Services School, CF Language School, SF Dental Services School, CF School of Intelligence and Security, CF Nuclear, Biological and Chemical School, CF School of Aerospace and Ordnance Engineer-

Above: Student firefighters extinguishing a blaze at the CFB Borden Firefighting Academy (CFFA). This is part of the regular training program laid out at this school. *DND PC-2224*

Left: CFFA Training at Borden is in all aspects of firefighting. Seen here are firemen just starting their attack on a simulated fire in a concrete building. *DND PC-1358*

ing, CF School of Instructional Technique, CF School of Physical Education and Recreation, CF Leadership Academy, CF Officer Candidate Detachment, Cadet Summer Training System and the Cadet Training Centre.

However, Borden's responsibilities went beyond those assigned to it by training system. It was also the host base for the Provincial Warning Centre and supported agencies that were responsible to other headquarters and commands. Of these perhaps the most important were the CF Ammunition Depot at Angus (an NDHQ asset), Communication Command's CF Data Centre and Force Mobile Command's Combat Maneuver Area and Combat Training Section. When these last two establishments were added to those of the CF Training System just under 117,000 man-days were devoted to training.

Perhaps the biggest moment of the decade came on 29 August 1979 when Barrie City Council granted CFB Borden "freedom of the city." A centuries old tradition, granting of this honour recognizes a special bond between a city and a military unit. Commanded by Colonel R.J. Ford, the commandant of the School of Administration and Logistics, a large contingent from Borden marched to Barrie city hall with "bayonets fixed" and "banners flying." Mayor Ross Archer, in granting freedom of the city, paid tribute to the long history of harmony and cooperation that existed between Barrie and Borden.

The 1980's would be another busy decade for Borden, but it started with a touch of controversy. In July 1981, the Atomic Energy Control Board of Canada announced that approximately 4000 tons of soil contaminated with small amounts of radium would be moved from the Malvern subdivision in Scarborough, Ontario, to the base for temporary storage. This did not please the surrounding communities. Demonstrations were held and petitions

organized while court injunctions were sought to prevent the move of the contaminated soil. Finally, eight months later, the Atomic Energy Control Board reversed their decision and the soil was sent to another locale.

Given the publicity surrounding the struggle the storage of nuclear waste, it seemed strangely appropriate when the Premier of Ontario, Bill Davis, and his ministers decided to hold a cabinet meeting in the Regional Emergency Government Headquarters bunker. A five hour meeting on 18 August 1982 was combined with a tour of Borden's emergency facilities that would come into play in the event of nuclear war.

The history Borden and the vicinity is rife with stories of weather related problems. In most instances it was dealing with an

text continued on page 87

An oblique aerial view of the CFB Borden hospital, looking east onto the west side of the building (building 0-166). *DND photo CBC00-1322*

Medical Branch badge

Dental Branch badge

Left: Cpl Tom Rocco working on a denture plate as Dental Lab Technician at the Dental Service School.

DND 1076-133

Below left: LAC T.W. Bears, a Medical Assistant at Camp Borden, applies a supporting bandage to the leg of LAC J.M. Lochnan, a Radar Technician from Station Edgar.

DND PC-2429

Lt Audette Bechard, a Nurse at the CFB Borden Base Hospital examines Patient, Pte Jeff Leavitt, CFB Europe.

DND 1081-101

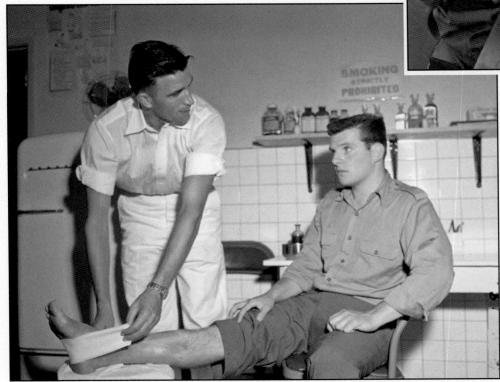

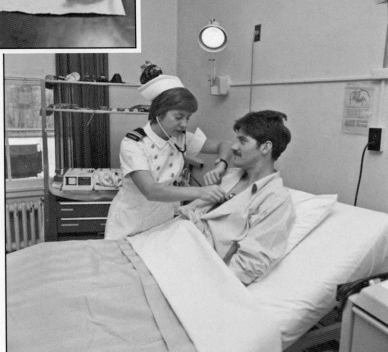

A Royal Canadian Air Cadets (RCAC) Schweizer glider over CFB Borden airfield. Borden hosted the nations first Air Cadet Gliding School in Canada in 1969 and although this moved to CFB Trenton in 1972, familiarization, or "fam", flights for the local RCAC squadrons continued to be a part of the Cadet Summer Training System programme at Borden. In later years the actual flight training would resume, ultimately becoming the Borden Cadet Flying Site, with the Schweizers and their Bellanca tugs in a smart new yellow and blue scheme.

DND I0C79-91

T-birds and Tutors, some with their former RCAF and CF serial numbers replaced by "A" series Instructional Airframe numbers (categorized to non-flying status), awaiting the attentions of Aerospace Engineering school instructors and students inside one of the newer hangers adjacent to Croil Hall. *DND RE70-1791*

This image provides a good snapshot of the aviation technical training area at Borden. With Croil Hall acting as the "school house" for classroom instruction, while most of the hands-on training is conducted in one of the two "new" hangars in the upper left hand corner. Serving as "gate guards" are a de Havilland Canada built CP-121 Tracker, an Avro CF-100 Canuck and a Canadair-built Sabre. *DND CBC00-352*

Pte Andrew Camacho and Steve Gallant working on a truck engine at CFB Borden. *DND photo IOC82-180*

An aerial view of the Base Transport Section complex. *DND photo IOC82-175*

Above: A 10 September 1975 oblique aerial of CFB Borden looking from the north side toward the south, with the vast Base Transport complex in the foreground — generally indicative of the Base's not insignificant logistics capability. *DND photo FA2010-1059*

Right: A circa April 1969 vertical aerial photograph of CFB Borden illustrating well the self-contained community that has grown larger than many of the small towns in this part of Ontario. *DND photo WG69-783*

exceptionally heavy snow fall or and early winter ice storm such as the one that struck the base on 16 October 1982. However, the loss of power for a short period of time and the need to clear up downed trees and branches paled in comparison to what transpired late in the afternoon of 31 May 1985. A series of tornadoes, including one rated as an F4 on the Fujita scale (with F5 being the strongest), ripped through the Allandale Heights area of Barrie and damaged five other adjacent communities. Within minutes eight people had died and a further 400 were injured. Hundreds of homes and business were either damaged or destroyed. For some reason the twisters missed Borden.

Once the extent of the damage became known units at the base sprang into action. Despite a base-wide power failure and a non-operational telephone system, the Base Commander, Brigadier-General J.I. Hanson, instituted a base recall using drivers to spread the word. In short order 700 personnel were gathered and dispatched to crisis centres to assist local authorities as required. Emergency supplies, such as beds, blankets, lanterns, flashlights, food and water, were gathered and made available. Military drivers and vehicles augmented community resources. Vacant base housing was made available to provide temporary shelter for some of the homeless. Although Borden continued to provide assistance in certain areas for many weeks to come, by 3 June the bulk of its personnel resumed their normal duties. It was a stellar example of one community lending a helping hand to its neighbours in a time of need.

text continued on page 91

The relationship between civil society and military organizations has not always been cordial. Cities and towns were often targeted in conflict as they were vital hubs of commerce, transportation and wealth. At times the privilege of "sacking" a city, where a conquering army was free to loot and pillage at will, was used in lieu of payment. As well, military force was often used to suppress the citizenry at the behest of rulers and governments. Therefore, it became common in practice and law to limit the presence of soldiers within the "walls" of a city.

However, if a bond of trust grew between a city and a unit or body of soldiers a special recognition of that bond could be bestowed. When the citizens granted the "freedom of the city" to a military unit, it could march within the city's walls with "drums beating, colours flying, and bayonets fixed." The awarding of the "key to the city" is a similar practice symbolically giving soldiers the key to unlock the community's protective gates. These are singular honours indicative of the trust that the people place in their military forces.

Today, the conveying of Freedom of the City or Key to the City normally recognizes the long history a Canadian Forces unit or organization has with a particular community. On 2 June 2012, the City of Barrie, Ontario, presented the Key to the City of Barrie to Canadian Forces Base Borden "to acknowledge and express its gratitude to the brave Men and Women of the Canadian Forces and to celebrate the deep and ongoing friendship between Borden and Barrie."

Capt Adele Boivin does a right dress after the command was given by Col S.E. Moore, CD, Parade Commander. On Saturday, 30 September 2006, The City of Barrie granted CFB Borden, The Grey and Simcoe Foresters, and 16 Wing, Freedom of the City. In the physical sense, this means the granting of the privilege for all time for a specific military unit to march through the city with "drums beating, colours flying, and bayonets fixed."

DND CB2006-0384-15

DND CB2006-0384-27

DND CB2006-0384-57

Top: The "Old Guard", The CFB Borden's Base Commander Colonel S.E. Moore, The Mayor of Barrie Robert Hamilton, Barrie's Chief of Police Chief Wayne Frechette, CFB Borden Base Chief Warrant Officer CWO J.O.F. Baillargeon all stand for a group photo in front of the Queens Hotel where one of the event's receptions was held. The ceremonial parade was held in Barrie, Ontario in front of City Hall.

Bottom: Troops marching up Collier Street led by the Pipes and Drums band.

All photos taken by Pte Samantha Crowe.

Borden Training & Support...

Reservist Pte Simon Jones of the Lorne Scots of Brampton (front) with rifle, and MCpl Joe Barta of the Lorne Scots of Oakville take up defensive position beside a bush during the reserve training exercise held at CFB Borden. *DND photo IOC88-165-8*

An infantryman training on a climbing part of the infantry obstacle course at Borden. *DND photo RE70-1783*

Members of 2 Airborne Medical Section, CFB Borden. L to R are Sgt G. H. McGillivray, Pte G. E. Mead and Lt. R. J. Hotchin. *DND photo PCN67-246*

Left: Cpl Gerry Martin, TQ 5 Student Cook prepares a decorated ham for a special food presentation. *DND photo IOC82-265*

MCpl Laurent Bergeron demonstrates preparation of trout to TQ 5 Cook Students. *DND photo IOC82-252*

Service men and women lined up at the steam tables at mealtime on base. *DND photo IOC82-159*

Exercise RITE CHOOSE - Engineers from No. I Troop lift with all their strength to release the pin from the ETP of the Medium Girder Bridge, during a disassembly procedure. *DND photo IOC90-8-53*

A soldier with his weapon slung on his back training on the ripline — a part of the obstacle course at Borden. *DND photo RE70-1776*

CFJLS outdoor activity in progress at CFB Borden in the mid 1970's. *DND photo PCN75-499*

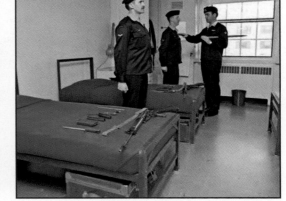

CFJLS trainees during a barracks inspection. *DND photo PCN75-472*

Below and opposite: When it comes to aircraft, even tasks that may appear mundane to the casual observer are done with precision and procedure. In most of these images Canadian Forces DHC-3 Otter No. 3671 (the photo immediately below shows Otter 3623) has its floats installed and inspected. CF School of Aerospace Ordnance and Engineering (later CFSATE) students learn all manor of minor and major procedures at CFB Borden. On this particular aircraft type, the floats could be "switched out" for wheeled landing gear, and skis could also be optionally installed on the main and tail wheels to cope with winter field conditions. Note the "cutaway" teaching aid CT-133 Silver Star, or "T-bird", in the back corner of the hangar in the top left photo opposite.

The internal landscape of Borden continued to change throughout the decade as older buildings were refurbished or replaced. A new $1 million CANEX storage facility was completed in 1981. The following year significant upgrades to the central heating plant commenced which eventually would see the elimination of a number of smaller boilers throughout Borden. The CF School of Administration and Logistics acquired a new headquarters and training building in 1985 and additional funds were provided to improve facilities at lodger units such as the CF Data Centre. As well, a Francophone school, École Joseph-Thomas Kaeble, named after a French-Canadian awarded the Victoria Cross in the First World War, officially welcomed its first students on 7 December 1982. However, at least for many of the younger members of the Borden family, perhaps the most welcome addition to "base infrastructure" was the opening of a McDonald's restaurant on 17 October 1982. No less a personage than Ronal McDonald was on hand when the first hamburger was sold to an appreciative member of the CF. A portion of the profits from the restaurant would go to support Non-Public Fund activities at Borden.

There were also a number of changes implemented within the training establishments. In 1985, one of the largest units on the base,

the CF School of Aerospace Ordnance and Engineering (CFSOAE) split into three separate facilities: the CF School of Electrical and Mechanical Engineers (CFSEME), CF School of Aerospace Technology and Engineering (CFSATE) and the CF Fire Academy (CFFA). These new institutions would be joined in 1987 by the CF School of Music (CFSM) that had transferred from CFB Esquimalt that summer. The following year the Minister of National Defence announced approximately $60 million worth of investment at Meaford. As part of the Land Reserve Modernization Project, a refurbished Meaford would become one of four Militia Training and Support Centres to be established across the country. Control of Meaford was transferred from CF Training Systems to Mobile Command in 1989.

As Borden approached the start of a new decade major changes were in the wind. The Cold War seemed to be coming to a close with the dismantling of the Berlin Wall. Internal chaos reigned in the former Soviet Union and Warsaw Pact countries where fast on the road to becoming democracies. The first faint whispers of a "peace dividend" could be heard in the halls of Ottawa. There was no doubt that Borden was about to embark upon a new series of adventures.

A Taurus Armoured Recovery Vehicle in Canadian Land Force United Nations markings during a CF School of Electrical and Mechanical Engineers (CFSEME) parade. *DND CBC94-457-18*

A Changing World

The first few years of the 1990's had brought about major changes in the world. Although the dissolution of the Soviet Union and the Warsaw Pact ended the Cold War, the world was still a dangerous place. Canadian military personnel embarked upon their first combat mission since the Korean War when the nation joined a coalition to oust Iraqi forces that invaded Kuwait in August 1990. Operation FRICTION, as the Canadian contribution in the Gulf War was called, became the first of a number of deployments that the CF would embark upon during the decade. Operating under the auspices of the United Nations, the North Atlantic Treaty Organization, and ad-hoc coalition, the CF experienced an unprecedented operational tempo.

At the same time economic and political factors combined to drive a series of resource reductions for the CF. The 1990's would see Canada's military forces shrink by almost one-third with a corresponding reduction in funding. These factors resulted in a decade-long restructuring and reorganization of the Department of National Defence and the CF. Borden would experience its fair share of these changes during this period.

In 1993, the base proper occupied approximately 51 square kilometres (31 square miles) and was responsible for a further 44 square kilometres (27 square miles) of territory at Meaford. Although a slew of wartime vintage buildings had been demolished between 1990 and 1992, there still remained 478 buildings and 1367 married quarters. In addition to the 12 integral CF training schools there were 19 lodger units including the CF Ammunition Depot (CFAD) at Angus. At the beginning of the decade the schools, plus support for the cadets and non-military agencies, amounted to the equivalent of 197,781 person-days of training. By 1994, this number fell to just under 129,000 with additional reductions to come.

The 1994 Defence White Paper resulted in a massive transformation of the Canadian Forces as the size of the military shrank with the disbandment of units, closure of bases and a restructuring of the command and control organizations. One of the first changes to impact Borden was the return of an "air force" presence with announcement that an Air Command wing would be established on the base.

Above: This 22 June 2009 photo by Sergeant Kev Parle provides an aerial view of CFAD Angus with the main CFB Borden complex (note the water tower) visible in the distance.

DND BM2009-2034-41

Right: Visitors from the People's Liberation Army Air Force (PLAAF) watching a demonstration of the marshalling simulator at the CFSATE at CFB Borden on 22 September 2006. The visitors included the Senior Class from the PLAAF Command College.

DND BM2006-0091-11

Authorized in May 1993, a formal parade commemorating the official stand-up of 16 Wing was held in conjunction with the CFSATE change of command event on 19 October 1994.

The Wing would be responsible to the Commander, Air Command, for a wide range of air-related training. With its headquarters in Croil Hall, 16 Wing administered three schools: CFSATE, the Air Force Professional Development and Training Centre (AFPDTC) and the CF School of Air Traffic Control (CFSATC). Concerned primarily with aviation technical training, CFSATE would focus on revamping the training necessary to support a rapidly changing 500-series trade structure as the air force modernized the way it approached maintenance and support. The AFPDTC, renamed the Air Command Academy in 2004, became responsible for providing professional development and leadership training to all levels of air force non-commissioned members. With the amalgamation of the Air Traffic Control and Air Weapons Control occupational fields, the CFSATC joined with the CF School of Air Weapons Control and Countermeasures in 1996 to become the CF School of Aerospace Control Operations (CFSACO). Although a 16 Wing unit, the CFSACO campus is located at the NAVCAN Training Centre in Cornwall, Ontario.

Upper right: Building S-114, the Propulsion Cell Training Facility on Ortona Road, is part of the CFSATE. This 16 Wing photograph was taken on 22 June 2009 photo by Sergeant Kev Parle. *DND BM2009-2034-56*

Lower right: The 16 Wing sign, on 19 October 2009 soon after it was repaired, located on Ortona Road just as you enter the Base from the Alliston Gate. *DND BM2009-2044-01*

MCpl Robert Ives demonstrates the SIMGRAPH trainer at the CFSATE on 30 Aug 06. MCpl Ives was demonstrating the system in preparation for a VIP visit. *DND BM2006-0082*

The air force presence at CFB Borden was strengthened further with the arrival of No. 400 Tactical Helicopter Squadron in 1996. A combined regular / reserve unit, 400 Squadron required a new home with the closure of CFB Toronto. By the end of the year, the squadron's CH-146 Griffon helicopters became a regular sight in the skies over the base and surrounding communities.

text continued on page 101

Ptes Shaun Gordon and Fabian Watson of the Jamaican Defense Force (JDF) pose under the canopy of a CT114 Tutor aircraft during their training at the Canadian Forces School of Aerospace Technology and Engineering (CFSATE). The JDF trains aircraft technicians at CFSATE.

DND BM2006-0116-02

Above: AVN Tech MCpl James McDonald from 8 AMS (Air Maintenance Section) Trenton and AVS (Aviation Systems Tech) MCpl Michael Bazalka, an from 12 AMS Shearwater, students on PLQ 0601, raising the flag at the Air Command Academy at CFB Borden.

DND BM2006-0023-11

Pte Michael Zebierre, an Aviation Technician (AVN Tech) student at CFSATE in 16 Wing Borden, practicing the disassembly of the canopy remover inside the cockpit of a CT-114 Tutor aircraft.

DND CBC01-0114

Another of the 22 June 2009 aerials... this view looks southeast over hangar No. 17 (left) and building A-171, the Stedman Building, a part of the CFSATE at 16 Wing, CFB Borden. The 'square' building in the centre back is the historic Croil Hall, the original postwar home of Air Force technical training on base.

DND BM2009-2034-31

Another of the 22 June 2009 aerials... looking northeast over building A-142, Croil Hall with the modified central heating plant in the upper part of the photo just right of centre and the rear of Hanger No. 17, with the two ground instructional airframe CH-113 Labrador in open-air storage on the hardstanding.

DND BM2009-2034-52

The CFSATE badge since 1989

An aerial view of the Air Command Academy Buildings S-136 (lower), & S-137 (left). Note the "gate guardian" CT-133, painted in a striking Red Knight aerial demonstration scheme.

DND BM2009-2034-66

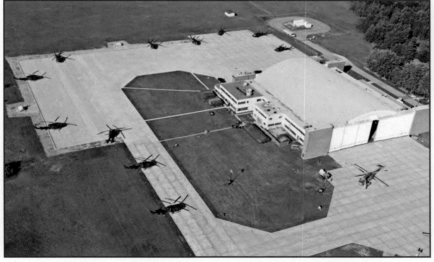

Above: An aerial view looking south over the flight line at CFB Borden. Hangar No. 18, used by No. 400 Tactical Helicopter Squadron (THS) is closest to the bottom of the frame, with a CH-146 Griffon helicopter parked on the hardstanding. The First World War era hangar row is visible in the centre of the photo. Some of the older structures are still standing while others have been replaced by more modern buildings. Only one of the original "triangle" of three runways remains.

DND BM2009-2034-22

Above and at left: A 20 June 2010 aerial view of helicopters from various squadrons on the flight line. No. 400 THS from Borden augmented by aircraft and personnel from 408 THS from Edmonton, 430 THS from Valcartier, 438 THS from St. Hubert, and 403 Helicopter Operation Training Squadron from Gagetown, was responsible for the tactical aviation portion of Operation CADENCE, the CF support to the G8 and G20 Summits. The CH-123A Sea King in the lower right of the photo, one of two present at the time, is a rare visitor to CFB Borden.

DND BM2010-2019-09 (left) & BM2010-2019-10

In this June 2007 photo taken near Gate No. 8 at CFB Borden with Naval Reserve Training Division-Borden students on the Rappel Master Course No. 0052 / 07, perform a six-person rappel from a No. 400 Squadron CH-146 Griffon helicopter.

DND CB2007-0232-05

DND CB2007-0232-08

Additional photos from the Rappel Master Course No. 0052 / 07:

At left, IPO2 J.C. Fiddler performs her practical objective check as a Rappel Master by securing Sgt B.A. Partridge and LS T.T. Ly onto the Griffon while Sgt A.M. Outar follows up with the Instructor final check of each students' rappel master potential.

At right, Sgt James J. Moore waits in position on the skid of the Griffon helicopter for the order to rappel, as Pte James A. Love, a student from Post Recruit Education and Training Centre (PRETC) who is tasked to support the Rappel Master Course, begins his descent.

DND CB2007-0232-40

Candidates of the Patrol Pathfinder (PPF) Course, Session 13, disembark from a CH-146 Griffon helicopter in the training area of CFB Borden on 28 July 2011. Session 13, which is headed by course director Capt Mover of Canadian Forces Land Advanced Warfare Centre (CFLAWC located at CFB Trenton), began on 16 May 2011 with 17 candidates, and is sixty training days long. The aim of the course is to enable Pathfinder personnel to execute insertion/extraction techniques by air, land, and sea in the context of adaptive dispersed operations in hostile environments; to enable personnel to perform the tactical marking and securing of a drop zone (DZ), landing zone (LZ), and beach heads, as well as airstrips used for tactical airlift operation for follow-on forces; and to enable qualified NCOs and officers to plan, coordinate, conduct, and advise commanders on PPF Operations. Photo by Cpl Katie Hodges.

DND CB2011-0215-02

It is 18 Dec 2008, and the 'Elves' ham it up prior to leaving to deliver the toys.(l-r) 'Brilliant' Cpl Marilou Langenhan, a Resource Management Support (RMS) Clerk, 'Candy Cane' Cpl Louise Davidson an Avionics Systems Technician (AVS) 'Ginger' MCpl Finton Moore a Supply Technician, 'Glitter' MCpl Susan Dorval an AVS, and 'Snow Flake' Pte Justin Hill who is awaiting training as an Aircraft Structures (ACS) Technician. 'Frosty' MCpl Clarence Shears, ACS Tech, is on the aircraft. No. 400 Squadron members raise funds throughout the year to purchase toys for kids who will be in Sick Kids Hospital in Toronto over Christmas. The toys are delivered by 'elves' via a CH-146 Griffon Helicopter. Photo by Sgt Kev Parle.

DND BM2008-2024-15

21 Feb 2009 Barrie, Ontario Photo by Sergeant Kev Parle View from the crane point of view of the slinging With the selling of the building previously owned by 441 Wing —of the Air Force Association, the T-33 Silver Star aircraft that was mounted on the pedestal there had to be removed and relocated back to Base Borden. The aircraft which was painted in the Red Knight paint scheme although showing tail # 21100 was in fact tail # CT133169. The Recovery and Salvage Support (RASS) Team from 8 Wing in Trenton was tasked to carry out the task.

DND BM2009-2008-21

As part of the ongoing transformation of the CF it was decided to create one command-level organization to be responsible for recruiting, education and training. Originally formed at CFB Trenton, the Headquarters, CF Recruiting Education and Training System (CFRETS) moved to Borden in 1995 and officially stood-up on 1 September 1996. A sub-formation of the Associate Deputy Minister (Personnel) in Ottawa, it would focus on recruiting and initial training for all ranks, as well as advanced training that was not the sole responsibility of one of the other Commands.

In order to meet the aggressive timelines for the establishment of this unit many of CFB Borden personnel were "double-hatted" serving as CFRETS staff personnel in addition to undertaking their normal base duties. A further rationalization of these duties led to the amalgamation of CFRETS and Borden staff under the banner of Commander Training Schools (CTS) in 1997. A little more than two years later CTS was reorganized and became the CF Support Training Group (CFSTG). With the disbandment of CFRETS in June 2002, many of its responsibilities were transferred to the CFSTG.

June 3, 2008 Canadian Forces Base Borden, Ontario Photo by Sgt Kev Parle Members of Canadian Forces Support Training Group (CFSTG) in Borden, do a group warm-up at the soccer field, before undergoing a 10 Km walk\run. The run was part of 'Run to Afghanistan', in support of our troops and the Canadian Forces (CF) Health and Physical Strategy. Canadian Forces Base Borden photo by Sgt Kev Parle.

DND BM2008-2001-01

To a lesser extent the reorganization amongst the command elements carried down to the training establishments. In 1997, Air Command's Aircrew Selection Centre moved to 8 Wing Trenton. That same year the CF Military Police and Security Academy split into the CF Military Police Academy and the CF School of Military Intelligence with the latter moving to CFB Kingston in the year 2000. However, Borden gained the Regional Cadet Support Unit (Ontario) with its transfer from Trenton that summer.

Even while in a constant state of organizational flux Borden was called upon to support ongoing CF operations. Throughout the decade individual personnel were called upon to support missions in such diverse locations as the Balkans, Africa and the Far East. In Canada, Borden was selected as one of the bases that would assist with the relocation of Kosovar refugees as part of Operation PARASOL. Finally, it was all hands on deck as Canada and the world prepared for anticipated wide-spread disruption of computer networks with the roll-over to the year 2000. Although Borden's military personnel spent several days on alert as part of Operation ABACUS in the end there were no major difficulties encountered.

text continued on page 104

Canadian Forces Base Borden has a long history of support for the Canadian Cadet organization. Whether it was the Army Cadets at Camp Ipperwash, Ontario, local Air Cadet squadrons, or Sea Cadet units parading in nearby communities, Borden was always ready to lend a hand with equipment, facilities and personnel. In 1994, the closure of Camp Ipperwash resulted in the establishment at Borden of the Blackdown Army Cadet Summer Camp. Located in a self-contained area of the base Army cadets spent their summer months under canvas while attending course of varying length. In 2003, the Army Cadet facility was amalgamated with the Borden Air Cadet Camp to form the Blackdown Cadet Training Centre. The new organization would focus on providing summer training for cadets from all three services. On any given year approximately 2000 young Canadians, ranging from 12 to 18 years of age, call Blackdown "home" for periods ranging from two to six weeks during the summer.

Borden Ontario photo by Aerial view of Blackdown Cadet Camp situated at Canadian Forces Base Borden. Photo taken 22 June 2009 by Sgt Kev Parle.

DND BM2009-2034-61

Capt Lorraine Guerreiro lands her RCAC Schweizer glider on 19 May 2010 when the Central Ontario Gliding Centre (COGC) held a Base Appreciation Flying Day. Representatives from the local media, as well as the members of various Base units, were taken on 15 minute flights.

DND BM2010-2014-12

Left: The A-152 Mess CFSTG Christmas mess dinner on 12 December 2005. Capt Pauline Quaghebeur, OIC BOR, serves Pte Samantha Crowe, CFSTG Image tech, with her Christmas dinner.

Right: A room inside the new Officer Quarters on CFB Borden — 7 April 2005.

DND CB2005-0560-14d

DND CB2005-0172-02d

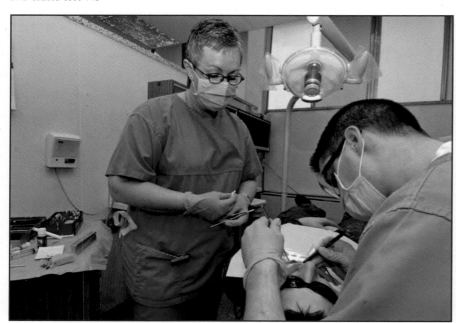

Capt Jeremy B. Blacquier, a Dental Officer from No. 1 Dental Unit Detachment, is assisted by Dental Technician, Cpl Debbie L. McKay as he performs root canal treatment on Pt Matthew K. Hatt, a student on the Soldier Qualification Course No. 0205 at Meaford in January 2006. The clinic is in Building O-114, CFB Borden.

DND CB2006-0019-10d

The entrance of the Canadian Forces Medical Services School/ Canadian Forces Dental Services School building in seen here in an 11 April 2005 photo.

DND CB2005-0124d

The terrorist attack on the World Trade Centre in New York on 11 September 2001 ushered in a new set of operational requirements for the Canadian Forces. Canadian military personnel found themselves tasked with supporting coalition operations in the Middle East and Afghanistan. The sheer size and duration of these commitments meant that the CF needed to draw personnel from units and bases across the country. Borden did, and still does, provide a number of personnel to flesh out Canadian operational formations as required. However, this meant that the base was chronically short of personnel for most of the first decade of the 21st century. Indeed Borden is still not up to full strength.

Through it all, Borden's military and civilian personnel stepped-up to the challenge of meeting the additional training requirements brought about by an increased operational tempo. Organizational changes continued as efforts were made to streamline and rationalize training. In 2002, CFRETS was disbanded effectively creating two distinct areas of responsibility: recruitment and education and training. Responsible for the latter, the CF Support Training Group (CFSTG), under the command of the dual-hatted CFB Borden base commander, was subordinate to the Assistant Deputy Minister,

Human Resources – Military (ADM (HR-Mil)). For the most part this command and control arrangement still exists today although the CFSTG is now called the Military Personnel Generation Training Group (2015) focusing primarily on military training and ADM (HR-Mil) has become the Chief of Military Personnel (CMP).

Changes to the various Borden-based units continued throughout the decade. The CF Dental Services School joined with the CF Medical Services School in 2003 to become the CF Health Services Academy responsible to the CF Medical Group. While in February 2007, responsibility for the CF School of Electrical and Mechanical Engineering, the CF School of Military Engineering and the CF School of Communications and Electronics was transferred to the Chief of the Land Staff (CLS). Later that year the Explosives Ordnance Disposal section of the CF School of Administration and Logistics was also transferred to the CLS. And in 2009, a course to introduce Aboriginal youth to the Canadian Forces welcomed it first intake. The Black Bear programme would continue at CFB Borden until 2012 when it was transferred to Gagetown, New Brunswick.

Borden continued to be heavily involved with the surrounding communities. Starting in 2003, No. 400 Squadron forged a strong

text continued on page 107

Buildings adjacent to the old airfield housing major elements of the Canadian Forces School of Electrical and Mechanical Engineering (CFSEME) at CFB Borden are illustrated in these two photos. The older brown brick, green roof block (foreground in the upper left photo) is Building A-141, home to the CFSEME Regimental Company while the more modern blue-grey structure (Building A-254) and the out-buildings on the same lot belong to the School's Vehicle Company.

DND BM2009-2034-24 & BM2009-2034-21

The CFSEME badge

CFSEME students work through a rigorous schedule on the Leopard C2 main battle tanks. They will be the next set of mechanics to maintain the fleet of Leopards.

DND LX2006-0333d

A LAV III rolls past during a CFSEME Change of Command Parade on 30 June 2005 at the Sicily Parade square. On the occasion, LCol Rod Berscheid took over from LCol Denis Carrier. The School Sergeant-Major changed from MWO Patrick Butler to MWO Jim Leal. Vehicle's from CFSEME join the march past. *DND CB2005-0270-52d*

Above: 13 March 2007 — On top of the Heavy Logistic Vehicle Wheeled (HLVW) Pte T. Harris mans the C9 Light Machine Gun (LMG), while Pte C.N. Melanson is in the driver's seat during Mobile Support Equipment Operator (MSE Op) Qualification Level 3 Course No. 0050. During the finial week in the field on this course, trainees do Convoy Operations for the first time. Convoy Operations are specific tactics, techniques and procedures that will assist in the conduct of operations and counter threats against convoys such as mines, improvised explosive devices (IED), suicide bombers and direct attack or ambush. *DND CB2007-0092-04*

Right: While on the same Course, Cpl Jamie M. Rubia and Pte Winston Gillam perform a "5 and 20 meter check" when the training convoy was brought to a stop for the third time. *DND CB2007-0092-64*

Above: Cpl Patrick Taillon "stands overwatch" during a Mobile Repair Team (MRT) scenario at the entrance of a vehicle hide. Cpl Taillon and his fellow CFSEME students were participating in the MRT exercise at CFB Borden on 29 March 2007. It came as a surprise for a lot of non-EME personnel in the Forces when, as of 1 April 2007, the CFSEME officially joined the Army. While it was rumoured that the establishment would pick up and move to CFB Gagetown, the school remained, and still remains, at CFB Borden for many years and many courses to come. *DND LX2007-0139d*

Right and bottom right: Getting a lift to the top, two soldiers from CFB Borden enjoy a day of snowboarding during the 20th Annual Mash Bash at Snow Valley Ski Resort. With a partnership between CFB Borden, Royal Victoria Hospital in Barrie Ontario and Snow Valley Ski Resort as the host for the 20th Annual Mash Bash. Skiing and snow boarding as the main activities, there was also TV's Mash theme games for everyone including the hill's favourite, the bedpan race. The days event raises approximately $25,000 annually for a total of $300,000 over the past 20 years. *DND LX2007-0091d*

As another bed pan race hurdles down the ski hill, Doo Doo the Clown gets the crowd cheering for their favourite racer. Skiers, snowboarders, corporate mascots and media celebrities all participate in this popular event within an event. *DND LX2007-0094d*

The Canadian Forces Medical Services School (CFMSS I, Building O-166, CFB Borden) looking from the southeast toward the northwest. Taken by Sgt Kev Parle on 13 February 2009 from No. 400 THS Griffon helicopter 146463, piloted by Capt Maurice Patenaude and Capt Terry Wong while delivering Col Guy Hamel CFB Borden / CFSTG Commander, and CWO Christian Thibault Base / CFSTG Chief Warrant Officer to the 22nd Annual Mash Bash. *DND BM2009-2005-05*

relationship with the Sick Kids Hospital in Toronto. Every year Operation HO HO HO saw members of the squadron deliver toys and holiday cheer to children and families at the hospital. Closer to home, the Canadian Forces Health Services Training Centre, supported by volunteers from throughout the Base, would continue to sponsor the yearly M.A.S.H. Bash. In conjunction with the Snow Valley Ski Resort in Barrie this event has, since 1987, supported local hospitals. In 2010, Barrie highlighted the close ties between the city and Borden with the start of the first step in creating an Historic Military Park on the south shore of Kempenfelt Bay. On 6 June 2010, with an honour guard from CFB Borden present, the city announced the first part of a multi-year plan to create a scenic area commemorating the close links that Barrie has had with the Canadian military over the years.

In August 2010, the Minister of National Defence, Peter MacKay, announced a fresh round of investment with $210 million allocated towards six separate projects. In addition to upgrading and consolidating select infrastructure items, a new CF Military Police Academy building was to be built and the design of a new CF recruiting headquarters commenced. The following year a further $77 million was allocated to build two new all-ranks kitchen and dining facilities. In August 2012, construction commenced on the new $13.75 million CF Recruiting Group headquarters.

If there has been one constant in the history of Borden it is that nothing stays the same and the past few years have been no exception. In July 2010, responsibility for the CFSACO was transferred from 22 Wing North Bay to Borden. The CF School of Administration and Logistics was given a name change in 2012 when it became the CF Logistics Training Centre. Ending an almost 40-year affiliation with Borden, the CF Language School closed its doors in 2013. And the Base proper was not left out of the equation as in 2014 Borden's Construction Engineering section was transferred to the Real Property Operations Group under ADM (Infrastructure and Environment).

There were also some significant firsts during this part of the decade. In May 2010, CWO David Fischer became the first Non-Commissioned Member to serve as Commandant of a major school when he takes command of the Air Command Academy. Col Tammy Harris also made history in 2012 when she becomes the first female Base Commander of CFB Borden.

Two events took place that brought home to all concerned the link between past and present. In 2011, a section of First World War training trenches were rebuilt by personnel from No. 32 Combat Engineer

text continued on page 114

This 26 September 2006 photo by Pte Samantha Crowe shows (left to right) CFSTG / CFB Borden CWO J.O.F. Baillargeon, CFSTG and CFB Borden Commander Col S.E. Moore, and the Mayor of Barrie, Robert Hamilton, raise the CFB Borden Flag in front of Barrie City Hall. *DND CB2006-0370-03*

Below: Remembrance Day, 11 November 2011. In this photo by Cpl Katie Hodges, spectators gather around to read the commemorative plaques and view the results after the unveiling of the First World War training trenches reconstructed at CFB Borden. Work on the project commenced on 3 August 2011 with a crew of eight military personnel from No. 32 Combat Engineer Regiment (32 CER) working for three days to construct the 15 meters of 1 meter wide by 1.5 meters deep "W" pattern zigzag trench. Construction was with the same tools used in 1916, without the use of heavy equipment or electricity. The final stage of the project included an opening ceremony on the day this photo was taken. *DND CB2011-0347-011*

On 9 February 2005, Bob Heatherington and Bob Housh from All Canadian Crane Rentals load the 35 ton German *Panther* (*Panzer V*, or Sd.Kfz.171) Second World War tank, from Worthington Park at CFB Borden, onto a flatbed using a 300 ton Demag crane for transport to Ottawa where the vehicle would then be put on display in the Canadian War Museum.

DND CB2005-0043-03d

Above: The tail section of a Northrop Nomad aircraft No. 3521 sits on the barge after members of the Royal Canadian Navy and the Royal Canadian Air Force raise it from the bottom of Lake Muskoka, Ontario, on October 28, 2014 . This former No. 1 SFTS aircraft had crashed into the lake after a mid-air collision with another Nomad on 13 December 1940. Photo by MCpl Roy MacLellan, 8 Wing Imaging. *DND TN-2014-0669-J0034*

The Base Borden Military Museum archway where the parade for the grand reopening of the museum took place on 9 June 2007.   *DND CB2007-0215-01*

An aerial view of the entrance to the Base Borden Military Museum Air Annex looking east, taken by Sgt Kev Parle on 22 June 2009. Pictured in front of the building (formerly hangar No. 11 of the First World War era "hangar row") is Avro CF-100 Canuck No. 18194 flanked by two CT-133 Silver Star (T Bird) aircraft of the museum collection.   *DND BM2009-2034-29*

The tri-trade monuments located at the north entrance to Canadian Forces Base Borden, taken on the 30 Aug 2005.   *DND CB2005-0371-02*

The Col Webb Building (Building S-149) houses the Food Services and Steward Training Company at CFB Borden.

DND CB2005-0531-01d

The finer side of the CFSAL Food Services & Stewards School training is pictured here — a delectable Shrimp with Italian Salad dish created in the French QL5 Cook Course No. 0026.

DND CB2005-0531-01d

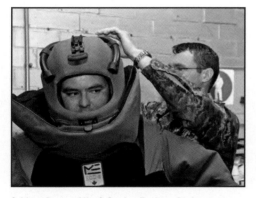

Cpl Ivan Peters of No. 2 Combat Engineer Regiment gets a hand suiting up in the Med-Eng EOD8 suit, which provides technicians with a balanced protection against the dangers of Explosive Ordnance Disposal (EOD) — overpressure, fragmentation, impact and heat. This type of training comes under the Canadian Forces School of Administration and Logistics located at CFB Borden. *DND LX2007-0760d*

The CF Logistics Training Centre badge

3....2...1...firing! And the car that was sitting peacefully downrange is now enveloped in a huge blast. When the dust settles and it is safe to approach the students of the Improvised Explosive Device Disposal Course will examine the remains of the vehicle to determine what has happened. The CFSAL is home to the EOD Training Centre, which is responsible for all training of Ammunition Technicians and also for Explosive Ordnance Disposal and Improvised Explosive Device Disposal courses. The Center also provides an on-call EOD Unit.

DND LX2007-0752d

A Terrorism Hazmat exercise for the Canadian Forces Fire Academy (CFFA). This particular exercise is of an NBC situation where a terrorist is in the area and there is a casualty. Cpl D. Gosselin and Cpl G.T. Hicks come in on a second round with more kit and to retrieve the casualty.   *DND CB2005-0133-12*

A dramatic group photograph of members on the QL3 Fire Fighter Course No. 0015 at the CFFA.
DND CB2007-0165

Tower 4 is one of several CFFA training buildings on the field. Photo taken by Cpl Charlotte McShane, CFSTG Imaging Base Borden.   *DND CB2006-0343-08*

Another training installation used by CFFA trainees is this odd looking "large baby aircraft" trainer.
DND CB2006-0343-022

The Billy Bishop Centre, home of the Canadian Forces Nuclear Biological Chemical (NBC) School, at CFB Borden.

DND CB2006-0090-01

LCol Jean J. Bourgeois, CD, says a few words before departing as Commandant of the Canadian Forces Chaplain School and Centre during the Change of Command Ceremony. LCol J.Y.R. Pichette, CD, Ph.D, assumed the role on Thursday, 28 June 2007 at the St-Joseph's Chapel (Building P-161) in CFB Borden.

DND CB2007-0255-03

The Outgoing Commodore J. Roger MacIsaac, CD, addresses guests at the CFRG HQ Change of Command Parade. The incoming CO at the time was Col Matthew K. Overton, CD. The Presiding Officer for the parade is Rear-Admiral Tyrone H.W. Pile, CD. The Parade was held at Cooper Hall, at the CFMSS Theatre, on 14 May 2007.

DND CB2007-0176-13

Inspection of the graduates of the Basic Military Qualification (BMQ) Course No. N0001 during an inspection of the Naval Reserve Training Division-Borden. The Reviewing Officer for the Graduation Parade is Captain (N) Jennifer J. Bennett, OMM, CD, who is also the Pacific Region Coordinator at the Canadian Defence Academy. The Graduation was held on Normandy Parade Square at CFB Borden on 28 June 2007.

DND CB2006-0253-05

The Chief of the Defence staff (CDS) General R. J. Hillier says a few words to Pte R.M.F. Whalen, a student awaiting her Qualification Level 3 Medic Course, during the 38th Birthday Celebration for Logistics and the 20th Anniversary of the Major-General M.L.Brennan Building in 2006. Furthermore, this was also the occasion of the ceremony to formally rededicate the CFSAL as the Home Station of the Logistics Branch and the first official visit by the CDS to speak to the men and women of both the Base and its various lodger units.

DND CB2006-0040 01

Regiment. Unveiled during the 11 November Remembrance Day ceremony the refurbished trench gives visitors a glimpse of how soldiers were trained back in 1916. Then in July 2012, the remains of a Second World War Nomad aircraft was found deep beneath the waters of Lake Muskoka. The aircraft from RCAF Station Camp Borden had crashed on 13 December 1940 after a mid-air collision with another aircraft and had lost until 2012. The crew of two were buried with full military honours at the Woodlawn Memorial Park Cemetery in Guelph, Ontario.

The CFB Borden of today occupies just under 8,500 hectares (21000 acres) inclusive of a 2,430 hectare (6,000 acre) training area. The 460 buildings on the base, with a few still under construction, span the 100-year history of the camp. Training is Borden's bread and butter. The approximately 3,250 military personnel and 1,500 civilian employees train an average of 15,000 students every year. It costs approximately $49 million dollars to operate Borden per year and, when combined with the almost $142 million in salaries, you can imagine how important the base is to the local economy.

For one hundred years Borden has been a key component of Canada's military. With a record of service, both to the country and surrounding communities, second to none the men and women who have served at Borden have carved out a unique niche in Canada's history. Imagine what Borden will accomplish in the next 100 years…

In 2015, the Base Commander, Colonel J.B.C. Doyon also became commander of the newly created Military Personnel Generation Training Group (MPGTG). The MPGTG is responsible for eight training establishments four of which are located at Borden. Between then they train approximately 16,000 military personnel annually. The units are:

- Canadian Forces Chaplain School and Centre
- Canadian Forces Fire and Chemical, Biological, Radiological and Nuclear Academy
- Canadian Forces Logistics Training Centre
- Canadian Forces Training Development Centre
- Canadian Forces School of Military Intelligence (CFB Kingston)
- Canadian Forces School of Meteorology (CFB Winnipeg)
- Canadian Forces Leadership and Recruit School (CFB St. Jean)
- Canadian Forces Language Schools (Various)

Canadian Forces Base Borden supports a number of additional training establishments and units that do not fall within the MPGTG chain of command. These units are:

- Canadian Forces Military Policy Academy
- Canadian Forces Health Services Training Centre
- Royal Canadian Electrical and Mechanical Engineers School
- Canadian Forces School of Aerospace Technology and Engineering
- Royal Canadian Air Force Academy
- 16 Wing
- Canadian Forces Ammunition Dump – Angus
- Canadian Forces Recruiting Group Headquarters
- 3rd Canadian Ranger Patrol Group
- No. 400 Tactical Helicopter Squadron
- No. 31 Canadian Forces Health Services Centre
- No. 1 Dental Unit
- Regional Post Office Detachment – Borden
- Civilian Human Resources Centre
- Deputy Judge Advocate – Borden
- Dispute Resolution Centre
- Integrated Personnel Support Centre – Borden
- Grey and Simcoe Foresters

CFB Borden, in winter, 2008.

DND BM2008-2025-01